CYBER SECURITY

Significant Issues Series

Timely books presenting current CSIS research and analysis of interest to the academic, business, government, and policy communities.

Managing editor: Roberta L. Howard

For four decades, the **Center for Strategic and International Studies (CSIS)** has been dedicated to providing world leaders with strategic insights on—and policy solutions to—current and emerging global issues.

CSIS is led by John J. Hamre, formerly deputy secretary of defense, who has been president and CEO since April 2000. It is guided by a board of trustees chaired by former senator Sam Nunn and consisting of prominent individuals from both the public and private sectors.

The CSIS staff of 190 researchers and support staff focus primarily on three subject areas. First, CSIS addresses the full spectrum of new challenges to national and international security. Second, it maintains resident experts on all of the world's major geographical regions. Third, it is committed to helping to develop new methods of governance for the global age; to this end, CSIS has programs on technology and public policy, international trade and finance, and energy.

Headquartered in Washington, D.C., CSIS is private, bipartisan, and tax-exempt. CSIS does not take specific policy positions; accordingly, all views expressed herein should be understood to be solely those of the authors.

The CSIS Press

Center for Strategic and International Studies
1800 K Street, N.W., Washington, D.C. 20006
Telephone: (202) 887-0200   Fax: (202) 775-3199
E-mail: books@csis.org   Web: www.csis.org

CYBER SECURITY

Turning National Solutions into International Cooperation

edited by James A. Lewis

foreword by Zoë Baird

THE CSIS PRESS

Center for Strategic
and International Studies
Washington, D.C.

Significant Issues Series, Volume 25, Number 4
© 2003 by Center for Strategic and International Studies
Washington, D.C. 20006
Printed on recycled paper in the United States of America
Cover design by Robert L. Wiser

07 06 05 04 03   5 4 3 2 1

ISSN 0736-7136
ISBN 0-89206-426-9

Library of Congress Cataloging-in-Publication Data
Cyber security : turning national solutions into international cooperation edited by
James A. Lewis ; foreword by Zoë Baird.
    p. cm. — (CSIS significant issues series ; v. 25)
    Includes bibliographical references and index.
    ISBN 0-89206-426-9 (pb : alk. paper)
    1. Computer networks—Security measures. 2. Cyberspace—Security
measures. I. Lewis, James Andrew, 1953- II. Center for Strategic and International
Studies (Washington, D.C.). III. Series: Significant issues series ; no. 4.
TK5105.59.C93 2003
005.8–dc21

                                                    2003004413

CONTENTS

FOREWORD

Zoë Baird

We live in an increasingly interdependent world. This is in large part the result of information and communications technology and its ability to forge new interconnections among people and nations. There are many benefits to this interdependence. But interdependence also means that governments face a new, difficult set of challenges. Among the most crucial of these challenges are the need to extend governance into digital networks, and the requirements of coordinating national solutions with other nations within a cooperative international framework.

In the last few years, policymakers have begun to recognize that new modes of governance are needed to address new technologies. To be effective, these new modes will need to emphasize cooperation, pluralism, and transparency among a broad range of actors, including other nations, private companies, and nonprofit organizations.[1] All of these actors will need to work together to craft forward-looking and innovative policies.

Cyber security is one important challenge that requires such new and cooperative policies. Individual governments, no matter how effective their national programs, cannot on their own provide the security that is so essential for digital networks to fulfill their promise. The challenges of cyber security will therefore require collaboration between nations, and this collaboration in turn will require new policies and forms of policymaking.

ZOË BAIRD is the president of the Markle Foundation.

For this reason, the Markle Foundation was pleased to support a meeting among five governments to look at the problems of cooperation in cyber security. The conference brought together senior representatives from the United States, Japan, Singapore, Hong Kong, and Australia to discuss the challenges—and opportunities—of ensuring cyber security in a global environment.

This volume represents the results of this undertaking. It collects essays by leading thinkers on Internet governance and provides insight into what key governments are doing to make the Internet more secure. More generally, as the outcome of a project that provided opportunities for contact and communication between states, it shows us that (and how) states can cooperate effectively to create models for effective policymaking and long-term change.

We at Markle intend to continue our work with others for fair and effective policies that serve the public interest in a networked world. The Joint Conference on Cyber Security and Transnational Collaboration and the volume that emerged from it are important steps in this process. The ability to repeat their success in bringing together new partners and finding new ways to work together will only grow in importance as we continue to move forward in taking on the urgent issues of building collaboration in a global society.

Note

1. See, for example, Zoë Baird, "Governing the Internet: Engaging Government, Business, and Nonprofits," *Foreign Affairs* 81, no. 6 (November/ December 2002): 15–20.

ACKNOWLEDGMENTS

This volume grows out of the work and expertise of many people. The focal point for their efforts was a joint conference on cyber security entitled "Providing Cyber Security in a Global Age," sponsored by the Institute of Defence and Strategic Studies, the Center for Strategic and International Studies, and the Markle Foundation.

The conference was attended by representatives from five governments, all of them involved in cyber security issues. Officials from Australia, Hong Kong, Japan, Singapore, and the United States participated fully and made extensive contributions. Katherine Zuback, a Department of Defense employee and then a CSIS visiting fellow, provided invaluable assistance. She and the other chapter authors have made valuable contributions. Two scholars who attended the conference, Michael McRobbie and Sy Goodman, deserve special thanks for their work and participation.

Ambassador Mushahid Ali and Ambassador Barry Desker played central roles in the organization and substance of the conference. Its success is due in large part to their efforts and to the work of the Institute of Defence and Strategic Studies in Singapore in hosting and cosponsoring the discussion.

None of this would have been possible without the support and active involvement of the Markle Foundation. Zoë Baird, president of Markle, helped shaped the broad themes and put them in the larger context of Internet governance. Stefaan Verhulst provided admirable support and was essential in the development of this volume.

Two people above all are responsible for the success of this effort. First, Stacey Murdock, CSIS Technology and Public Policy Program coordinator, did the work of an entire embassy in organizing a conference on the other side of the world from Washington. Coordinating closely with the Institute of Defence and Strategic Studies and officials in five governments over many months, she dealt superbly with all of the requirements of a multicultural effort. The flawless conference and the follow-up that resulted in this volume are due to her tireless and skillful work.

Finally, John Hamre, president and CEO of CSIS, is responsible for the intellectual framework that led to this volume and was the chief motor for driving the discussion. His active involvement provided a focus and a depth that otherwise would not have been possible.

INTRODUCTION

James A. Lewis

The Internet is a vast, anonymous agglomeration of open computer networks. It is international, and it is vulnerable. Improving the security of this global collection of networks will require cooperation among countries.

The shape and nature of this cooperation is only now beginning to emerge from discussions in a range of bilateral and multilateral settings. The chapters in this volume are based on the assumption that to build cyber security, countries must develop and implement competent domestic strategies and must also find ways for effective cooperation with other nations.

CYBER SECURITY AS A NATIONAL AND INTERNATIONAL ISSUE

Contrary to the early pronouncements of various Internet gurus, cyber space is not borderless. It has, in fact, many borders. These borders greatly complicate national efforts to secure networks. Governments are hampered by the multitude of borders because they are more constrained (and face higher costs) in regard to pursuing attackers outside of their jurisdiction. Most sovereign states view the intrusion of another state into their territory as an illicit or outrageous act, and a resident of one country need not heed the laws or police of another. In this sense, the Internet and cyber space are no different than any other national activity.

This is not a new problem. Countries have solved it in numerous other areas involving security and economies by developing cooperative arrangements that specify how countries will support one another and under what conditions one sovereign state will enforce the laws of another. The Internet does not yet have the web of cooperation that has been built up elsewhere. This is in part because it is new, in part because we are not sure what is needed, and in part because it infringes on so many sensitive issues of economic competition and national security.

Cooperation in cyber security is crucial because there are no national solutions to transnational problems. Hackers in one country can easily use the Internet to commit crimes in another. Their attacks, in fact, may use computer networks in several countries en route to their target or targets. A virus launched in one country can spread rapidly around the globe, infecting networks in dozens of nations. Although nations can take many steps to improve cyber security domestically, critical information networks are linked across national borders. Cooperation with other countries must be a central part of building cyber security.

A larger set of social, economic, and political changes has compounded the problem. Technological and political changes have enabled the greater interconnection (and ease of interconnection) among countries, firms, and persons. Market forces continue to make networks and infrastructure in different countries more interdependent and more linked. Financial and banking networks, telecommunications, and international aviation communications and traffic control are leading examples of larger, international networks on which the international economy depends but which no single country controls. Countries have had to adjust and readjust their policies to better manage the pressure interconnectedness puts on security and on economies.

The result is that, despite its many advantages, life in cyber space remains somewhat Hobbesian, not in the sense that it is "nasty, brutish, and short," but in that the rule of law does not extend very far. Although some in the Internet community prefer this, the result is a diminution of trust and security that limits the economic benefits of networks and creates new vulnerabilities for individuals, companies, and nations. To fulfill their central roles as guarantors of security and public order, governments will inevitably need to extend their activities into cyber space.

International cooperation comes in many forms and occurs at many levels, but cooperation on security matters is the most delicate. Security cooperation can be complicated when partners in security are also economic competitors. The degree to which partners share common values and goals shapes and sets the limits for cooperation in security. The threshold for cooperation is lower in commercial matters and law enforcement. The implications of this for cyber security are that cooperation between countries who are already partners (or allies) in other security or political matters will be easier and fuller, but that cooperation will be possible among countries that are not security partners for those aspects of cyber security that can be cast as commercial or law enforcement issues. International cooperation in cyber security might take place, then, simultaneously in several different venues, with cooperation in the Asia Pacific Economic Council (APEC) taking one form and cooperation in NATO taking another.

National governments will need to take the lead in building cooperative relationships. While there is a larger debate about the appropriate role for governments in Internet governance, with many advocating a limited role, the state has many essential advantages over the private sector in the areas of multilateral cooperation and cyber crime. Internet governance has largely espoused an ideal of a "nongovernmental, bottom-up, consensus-driven, self-organizing structure" that would emerge from the private sector in a process of self-regulation or self-governance. As Internet use becomes further integrated into national activities, however, complete reliance on self-regulation will be inadequate.

Internet governance came of age when many countries were well advanced in dismantling their government's role as the central manager of economic activity. The collapse of central planning and communism, the decade-long trend in industrialized nations toward deregulation (particularly in telecommunications), the disenchantment with Keynesian economic theory, and the euphoria of the tech-stock-market bubble all contributed to a notion that governments should stay out of Internet governance as much as possible. Yet, even though deregulation is essential for economic growth, it was inappropriately applied to the entire range of public policy problems generated by the Internet.

For certain public problems, government action, however messy, is more likely to produce good outcomes than a reliance on the private sector. Security is among the foremost examples of such public problems, and nations have always taken the primary responsibility for maintaining security against foreign threats and domestic order. In this sense, the Internet and cyber space are no different than any other national activity.

Moreover, while national efforts can improve cyber security, they must be complemented by bilateral or multilateral efforts. It will not be possible to build more secure networks unless sovereign states find ways to cooperate. At a minimum, the private sector cannot create or enforce laws. If an effective legal structure for cyber crime will deter attacks, the role of government is central, and if this is to work for a global network, this role must include a way to cooperate with other governments in enforcing laws.

CYBER SECURITY AND LAW ENFORCEMENT

Much of the early work on the "cyber threat" speaks of exaggerated risk and conflated threats in an unhelpful manner. It depicts hackers, terrorists, foreign spies, and criminal gangs who, by typing a few commands into a computer, can take over or disrupt the critical infrastructure of entire nations. This frightening scenario is not born out by statistics. No critical infrastructures have been shut down by cyber attacks. To date, cyber terrorism has been more like cyber graffiti, with groups defacing each other's Web sites.

Cyber attacks are far less damaging than physical attacks, and the risk to national security from cyber attack is low. For example, some analysts worry about cyber terrorists shutting down the national electrical power system. The United States has run, inadvertently, a large-scale test on the effects of disrupting the grid that suggests that this threat is exaggerated. When California revised its regulation of the state electric power market, the result was repeated blackouts and brownouts. Despite the increased cost, firms and individuals in California rapidly adjusted and the effect on the rest of the nation was minimal. Hackers would be hard pressed to match California's self-inflicted shutdowns, which suggests that even if computer attacks could disable parts of the electric power grid, the result would not be catastrophic.

A more dangerous approach would be a cyber attack in concert with a physical attack. For example, a cyber attack that turned off a local 911 system shortly before an explosion could compound the damage. Cyber terrorism and cyber crime could also overlap in damaging ways; groups could steal credit card numbers or important data to damage economies and for their own gain. The cost of cyber crime for individual firms (and, cumulatively, for national economies) continues to rise. The lack of security on the Internet also has implications for espionage and warfare. A sophisticated opponent might hack into a system and sit there, unobtrusively collecting intelligence or planting code that could be activated in a conflict.

Recovering from this era of "the-sky-is-falling" analysis requires us to put cyber security into perspective. Cyber security reflects a kind of amorphous threat that is difficult for the traditional tools of national security to reach. The lines between domestic and foreign, private and public, and police and defense are blurred. It is difficult, especially in the early stages of an incident, to determine if the attacker is a terrorist, group, foreign state, criminal, or teenager in Mendocino California. A quick survey of incidents over the last four years, however, suggests that criminals and bored teenagers are the most likely sources of attack. Cyber attacks, like bank robberies, are not a matter for national security. Cyber security is primarily a problem for public safety and law enforcement.

Localized law enforcement is at a disadvantage in an interconnected world, however. Law enforcement authorities are limited by jurisdiction—the geographical area to which authorities apply—and by sovereignty—the right of a group of people to govern themselves. The diplomatic tools developed for police in one country to request the assistance of police and courts in another—such as mutual legal assistance treaties (MLATs)—are slow and can be unhelpful if national laws are incompatible. Many countries still lack an adequate legal framework for the deterrence and punishment of cyber crimes or they rely on an uneven patchwork of legislation. International cooperation on cyber crime has been hampered by disagreement over what constitutes a crime; by inadequate, uneven, or absent authorities by which governments can investigate and prosecute cyber crime; and by lengthy procedures for international cooperation.

Sovereignty concerns are the largest obstacle to cooperation in cyber space. This problem is not insoluble. At some level, even political opponents are willing to cooperate on issues of law enforcement and public safety. Building cooperative arrangements among national agencies that allow for coordinated activities and information sharing can help ensure that the forces of globalization work for safety, not against it. The development of adequate and equivalent national civil and criminal laws for cyber space will also help build international cooperation.

CYBER-SECURITY COOPERATION IN A REGIONAL CONTEXT

The Asia-Pacific region illustrates some of the challenges international cooperation in cyber security may face. Except for ANZUS (Australia–New Zealand–United States Security Treaty) and the Five-Power Defense Arrangement, which are the result of much earlier efforts by the United States and United Kingdom, region-wide multilateral security arrangements have been unattainable in Southeast Asia since the days of SEATO (Southeast Asia Treaty Organization). The members of ASEAN (Association of Southeast Asian Nations) have engaged in a slow, incremental process to include security issues in the group's work, and the ASEAN Regional Forum (ARF) provides the only multilateral venue for the discussion of regional security issues.

This reflects long-standing regional tensions and competitions that shape the possibilities for cooperation in cyber security. Although cyber security is often presented as a national security issue, it could be better addressed as an economic and law enforcement issue. The basis for cyber security cooperation in the Asia-Pacific region may instead lie in strong multilateral economic cooperation and in several strong bilateral security relationships (usually with the United States as one of the partners). A cooperative approach to cyber security that emphasizes economic and law enforcement issues (rather than defense policy) and that rests on strong bilateral ties might work best in the Southeast Asian context.

Still another element that will shape regional cooperation in cyber security is participation in extraregional multilateral organizations. Many ASEAN countries and states are also members of the OECD (Organization for Economic Cooperation and Development) and the ITU (International Telecommunication Union), organizations that have cyber-security initiatives. The work of these larger groups will provide a broader framework for cooperation on regional levels. Cooperation among different multilateral groups will probably result more from overlapping membership (e.g., one country in several different cooperative relationships) than from new bilateral arrangements.

CONSTRAINTS ON COOPERATION

In reading the chapters that follow, it will be useful to keep the following questions in mind:

- How great is the scope for international cooperation outside of law enforcement cooperation?
- How much international cooperation is possible (or desirable) in "critical infrastructure protection"?
- How formal or structured do government actions need to be to promote cyber security both nationally and internationally?

Five membership groups account for most of the work on multilateral cooperation on cyber security. These are clustered among developed countries where cooperation on economic and trade issues (including crime) is already well developed and where network use is common and growing rapidly:

- The **Council of Europe,** as part of its larger efforts to harmonize criminal law and human rights within Europe, adopted its Cybercrime Convention, and it continues to work on cyber-crime issues.

- The **European Union** has begun an initiative in the context of its broader "Information Society and Freedom, Security, and Justice" program to improve the security of information infrastructures and combat cyber crime.

- The **Asia-Pacific Economic Council** (APEC) has endorsed a program to build cyber-security and critical infrastructure protection among its members.

- The **Organization for Economic Cooperation and Development** issued voluntary guidelines in August 2002 to improve the security of networks after the terrorist attacks in the United States. The OECD hopes that these guidelines to counter cyber terrorism, computer viruses, hacking, and other threats will promote international cooperation despite being nonbinding.

- The **Group of 8** (G-8) adopted an action plan for high-tech and computer-related crime in 2000 that included measures to facilitate mutual legal assistance among members, including a 24-hours-a-day, seven-days-a-week network of experts to assist in high-tech crime investigations. The program has now been extended to include a number of other countries.

The progress of these groups can be measured by looking at the complexity of their interactions. The simplest elements of effective cooperation are some agreement to voluntary, nonbinding national measures similar to the OECD's guidelines. A more complex level of cooperation would include information sharing among governments or CERTs (Computer Emergency Response Teams) and informal cooperation in the enforcement of national laws. APEC has taken measures like this. Complex interactions would be binding, entail frequent transactions, and involve some commingling of sovereignty such as is found in the G-8, with its common rules and undertakings, agreement on joint actions, and establishment of multilateral groups or task forces. The highest level of cooperation would involve exchanging legally binding commitments and obligations, where nations essentially surrender a part of their sovereign rights via a commitment to joint action with another nation or group of nations. A set of well-defined circumstances for this is found only in the Council of Europe Cybercrime Treaty.

The most active international cooperation for cyber security has been in law enforcement. Outside of law enforcement, however, there has been little progress in international cooperation. Cooperation among CERTs and in research and development efforts are useful areas, but given the large degree to which cyber security is a problem of crime and enforcement, the best area for cooperation may continue to be law enforcement. This has been the case with other transnational crimes, like money laundering and narcotics, and the next step for cooperation may be an effort like the Financial Action Task Force (FATF), a group established by the G-7 that has expanded to 31 members and observers and that has developed recommendations and vehicles for cooperation in fighting financial crimes.

Critical infrastructure protection has a strong law enforcement component, but goes beyond this to raise issues of national security. Nations would regard physical attacks by foreign entities on critical infrastructure as acts of war or terrorism, so critical infrastructure protection creates a new set of problems for national security. Cooperation on national security issues is more difficult to achieve among disparate nations—there is always the question of how much one wants to advertise vulnerabilities to potential opponents. Many critical infrastructures are also national in scope—electrical grids, water supply, emergency services, and government operations do not extend across borders. It may be easier to achieve international cooperation in critical infrastructure protection by starting with those areas where the transnational connections are very large, as in financial services. In other areas, it is possible that the chief interest for the United States may be to enhance international stability by helping other countries to recognize the need to protect critical national infrastructures. This type of cooperation may not require the level of formal agreement and commitments that are necessary for law enforcement cooperation.

This question—the degree to which government actions need to be formal and binding—has larger implications for the entire question of cyber security on both a national and international level. On a national level, prescriptive regulations that lay out in precise detail the steps private firms must take and the technologies they must employ are likely to be counterproductive and risk becoming technologically outdated. This does not mean that there is no scope for regulation, and it is fair to ask, after five years of calling for voluntary approaches to cyber security that never quite seem to emerge, whether governments need to consider measures, including regulation, that will motivate private actors to improve security.

On an international level, it is worth asking if the type of cooperation among nations needs to be the same for different kinds of cybersecurity problems. Some problems may be best solved through informal cooperation, such as information exchange among CERTS, while other problems, like those of law enforcement, may require more formal, binding agreements. Some areas, such as cooperation among private sector groups, may require only minimal government involvement; other problems may require governments to play a central role.

Formal, binding action is difficult to obtain among nations, especially on a multilateral basis, and to date most cooperation in cyber security has been informal and not legally binding. One sign of progress in international cooperation in cyber security will be the movement of multilateral cooperative activities into formal and binding arrangements. Current examples of cooperation include:

- *Formal bilateral*   MLATs
- *Informal bilateral*   Police contacts; CERTs
- *Formal multilateral*   Council of Europe
- *Informal multilateral*   Group of 8 (G-8); OECD; APEC; CERT collectives

FEATURES OF COOPERATION

The chapters in this volume, written by authors in Europe, the United States, and Asia, describe the predominant features of particular approaches to a transnational problem and examine the elements essential for success. The chapter authors come from diverse backgrounds—government, academia, and the private sector—and they draw on a considerable breadth of experience in law, negotiation, and technology.

The first chapter, by Michael Vatis, then director of Dartmouth College's Institute for Security Technology Studies, looks at informal cooperation at the bilateral level and discusses successful efforts at informal cooperation within the Group of 8. Vatis points out that, at least in this initial phase, it has been more effective to pursue informal cooperation on a bilateral basis for practical reasons (informal mechanisms are faster) and because of the sensitivity of some issues and the difficulty in distinguishing between events caused by criminals (cyber crime) and events caused by states (information warfare or espionage). Over time, however, Vatis believes that countries will move to more formal, multilateral modes of cooperation.

Next, Henrik Kaspersen, director of the Computer-Law Institute at the Vrije University in Amsterdam (and the author of the report on cyber crime for the Council of Europe that led to the Cybercrime Convention), looks at the Cybercrime Convention as a vehicle for treaty-based international cooperation and mutual legal assistance. Although he sees the Cybercrime Convention as an important vehicle for cooperation, Professor Kaspersen notes that it will need a variety of supporting measures to be fully effective. These could include measures to promote law enforcement cooperation and global programs to increase user awareness of network vulnerabilities.

Pottengal Mukundan, director of the International Chamber of Commerce's Commercial Crime Services, looks at the Piracy Reporting Center of the International Maritime Bureau. This privately funded informal network for dealing with a transnational criminal activity provides useful precedents for cyber security. Captain Mukundan proposes that the collection and dissemination of information on cyber attacks be carried out by a trusted, neutral, private-sector entity, as the Piracy Reporting Center does for piracy activities.

Robert S. Litt, a former official at the U.S. Departments of State and Justice now at Arnold and Porter, and Gordon N. Lederman, also at Arnold and Porter, examine the benefits of formal bilateral coop-eration in cyber security. Such agreements are often easier to obtain than multilateral agreements while providing more benefit than in-formal arrangements. Litt and Lederman note that formal mecha-nisms are probably essential to ensure that evidence gathered in one country is useable in the courts of another and that there are legal procedures for arrest and extradition.

Charles Lim Aeng Cheng, of the Attorney General's Chambers of Singapore, discusses the value of multilateral agreements, noting that it would be difficult for governments to develop a comprehensive net-work of bilateral agreements. That said, Lim urges a realistic ap-proach that recognizes that the digital divide among nations may slow the multilateral process.

Seymour E. Goodman of the Sam Nunn School of International Affairs and the College of Computing at the Georgia Institute of Tech-nology looks at the characteristics and difficulties of a treaty-based, multilateral approach to cyber security. Professor Goodman's chapter outlines what an ideal international arrangement would look like.

Stefano Rodotà of the University of Rome discusses the European legal framework for data protection and privacy, its implications for cyber security, and requirements and issues with multinational regula-tory tools. Professor Rodotà argues that cyber-security measures must be balanced against the "fundamental right" to data protec-tion.

My own chapter looks at the Council of Europe Cybercrime Con-vention in terms of the international public response and some of the differences in national legal systems and sovereignty issues that can impede formal multilateral cooperation. Chief among these are the differences between countries with a common-law background (in particular the United States) and those with legal systems based more on the Napoleonic Code. The Council of Europe Cybercrime Convention was able in most cases to negotiate solutions that allow the two systems to work together. Future efforts, particularly in regard to content (such as the work on "racist and hate speech") will face difficulties that may be insurmountable: most countries have no equivalent to the U.S. Constitution's First Amendment and its absolute right to freedom of speech.

Nobuo Miwa of Japan has written an informed discussion of the requirements for cooperation in cyber security, focusing on measures to collect information and identify vulnerabilities. Professor Miwa emphasizes the importance of government support for cyber-security efforts and cooperation with private companies in those efforts.

The volume concludes with a chapter by John Hamre, the president and CEO of CSIS, Prakash Abegaonkar, the president of the Bridging Nations Foundation and a senior associate at CSIS, and Katherine Zubeck of the U.S. Department of Defense, then a visiting fellow at CSIS. The authors look at cyber security as a transnational governance issue. Their chapter provides a broad framework for cyber security and discusses requirements for effective transnational governance, beginning with the need for effective domestic cyber-security programs and models for transnational cooperation.

CONCLUSION

There has been considerable progress in building cooperation on cyber security among some (but not all) countries. But much more can be done. This is not surprising. Countries and multilateral organizations have only begun to explore cooperation in cyber security. It is part of the larger trend to accommodate the new global networking technologies in the larger framework of international governance. The new global economic, political, and technological forces do not mean the demise of the state. Nevertheless, governments that fail to adapt their practices, including their modes of international cooperation, to accommodate and shape transformational economic and technological changes will only suffer as a result.

CHAPTER ONE

INTERNATIONAL CYBER-SECURITY COOPERATION

INFORMAL BILATERAL MODELS

Michael Vatis

Despite the bursting of the "Internet bubble" and the demise (at least temporarily) of the "dot.com" economy, Internet use continues to grow exponentially around the globe. This growth has been accompanied by a steady increase in the number and severity of "cyber attacks."[1] For instance, the Computer Emergency Response Team Coordination Center (CERT/CC) at Carnegie-Mellon University in Pittsburgh, Pennsylvania, a U.S. government–funded incident-handling entity, reported that the number of security incidents reported to it by private-sector companies has doubled each of the last two years from the year before.[2] And the Computer Security Institute's Computer Crime and Security Survey for 2001 found that "the threat from computer crime and other information security breaches continues unabated and ... the financial toll is mounting."[3] Computer Economics estimates that over the last few years, destructive viruses and worms have caused damage estimated in the billions of U.S. dollars worldwide.[4] For instance, Computer Economics estimates a total worldwide impact of over $30 billion over the last two years in "clean-up" costs and lost productivity.[5] Even if one discounts these figures substantially, the rising trends and the growing costs from computer crime are apparent from all available indicators.

Given the global nature of the Internet, it is not surprising that computer crime is also global, with attacks crossing national lines with increasing frequency. Operational efforts to prevent and respond to computer attacks must therefore also be global.[6] Attacks often originate in one country and pass through computer networks in several other countries before hitting their target in yet another country. This means that evidence necessary to trace an attack back to its source and identify the perpetrators might be found in several countries. Because there is no automated or easy way to trace an attack from the victim computer back to its source directly, law enforcement must typically trace an attack one step at a time, from one computer to the next, relying either on the cooperation of the owners of the affected systems or on compulsory legal processes within each country involved. Since no country to date has been willing to allow another country to conduct a unilateral investigation on its own soil (either physically, with agents from Country A on the ground in Country B, or "virtually," with investigators in Country A remotely conducting searches and forensic examination of computers in Country B through technical means), international cooperation among law enforcement agencies is critical.[7]

To date, the most effective mechanisms for international cooperation in dealing with cyber attacks have been informal and bilateral in nature. This is largely the result of a process of elimination—that is, informal arrangements have been relied on because of the relative unavailability or ineffectiveness of formal bilateral arrangements and the lack of either formal or informal multilateral conventions on operational cooperation.

Formal bilateral arrangements for information sharing, generally embodied in Mutual Legal Assistance in Criminal Matters Treaties (MLATs), do not exist between all of the countries that might need to cooperate on a cyber crime investigation. The U.S. State Department, for instance, reports that the United States has MLATs in force with only 19 countries (with another 15 signed but not yet ratified by the U.S. Senate or the other country. (See http://www.travel.state.gov/mlat.html.) Second, many MLATs do not cover computer crimes (either specifically or through broadly applicable general terms). And third, the procedures set out in MLATs typically are time consuming and somewhat burdensome.[8]

This last point might not be a significant problem for traditional, "physical crimes," where physical evidence (such as a document, a weapon, a piece of clothing, etc.) can be preserved until the formal legal procedures are completed. By contrast, a delay can pose an enormous—and irremediable—problem in computer crime cases because of the transient or perishable nature of digital evidence. Internet service providers and system administrators of networks are always looking to discard unneeded information in order to save storage costs, meaning that if digital evidence (such as historical transaction data or "log" information recording certain network activity) is not located and preserved quickly, it might be lost for good by the time formal procedures are completed. Alternatively, sophisticated hackers might succeed in going back into a network and erasing the digital trail if they suspect that law enforcement is onto them. The typical delays incurred by following formal procedures can therefore prove fatal to an international cyber investigation.

On the multilateral front, multilateral conventions (either formal or informal) have proven very difficult to arrive at in this area, for a number of reasons. One significant reason is that the growth of computer crime has affected different countries at different rates, meaning that many countries have not yet (or until recently) had to face the problem in a serious way. Indeed, many countries still do not have substantive criminal laws in place to address computer crime. These countries are therefore ill prepared to enter multilateral negotiations when they have not even addressed the problem internally.

A second reason for the dearth of formal multilateral conventions on cooperation is the difficulty of distinguishing some "cyber crime" from "information warfare" and cyber espionage. Nation-states can use the same basic techniques (or more sophisticated versions of the same) as hackers or cyber criminals as a means to attack another country's computer-controlled critical infrastructures (such as electrical power, telecommunications, or financial networks) in a time of war, or as a means of acquiring intelligence from government or civilian computer networks. Yet, in the early stages of an attack, it is difficult to distinguish a mere cyber crime from a case of cyber espionage or information warfare.[9] Given the growing number of countries that are developing cyber techniques for intelligence or warfighting purposes,[10] this is an increasingly complicated issue.

Imagine, for instance, that Country A experiences an intrusion and theft of sensitive high-tech information from a company or government agency, and it traces the intrusion back to Country B. It is possible that a criminal organization in Country B (or Country C) might be responsible, and that Country B might be willing to assist Country A. But it is also possible that an intelligence agency in Country B was responsible and that Country B might therefore not be willing to assist Country A. This is just one possible permutation.[11] Given the different national interests at stake in this area, and the suspicions that attend relations among some countries when it comes to intelligence and military matters, many nations undoubtedly would find it difficult to sign on to a multilateral convention that might bar them from engaging in activities that they would like to perform in the interest of their own national security.

One *informal* multilateral effort that has proven to be successful in this area is an initiative of the G-8.[12] This effort has succeeded largely because of the relative modesty of its goals, the small size of the group, and the commonality of interests. The G-8 Subgroup on High-Tech Crime was formed in January 1997[13] and has met numerous times since then. (This conference is fortunate to have as one of its participants Christopher Painter, the deputy chief of the Computer Crime and Intellectual Property Section of the U.S. Department of Justice and the new chair of the G-8 Subgroup on High-Tech Crime.) One of the principal successes of the subgroup has been the establishment of a "24/7" (24-hour/7-day-per-week) network of law enforcement points-of-contact for high-tech crime matters, including cyber crime, in each of the G-8 countries. That network has since been expanded to include a number of non-G-8 countries and is in the process of being expanded further. The network has been successful in fostering speedy communications between and among member countries, allowing for the quick preservation of perishable digital evidence until legal processes can be taken to provide formal assistance.

The G-8 Subgroup has also hosted an international training conference to train law enforcement officials from member countries on investigating computer crimes, and it has collected and reviewed the G-8 member countries' respective laws concerning computer crime. In addition, it has hosted meetings between law enforcement and industry representatives, including representatives from hardware manufacturers, telecommunications carriers, and Internet service providers (ISPs). These meetings have addressed concrete steps law enforcement and industry can take to improve cooperation between the two sectors; develop technical standards that take into account public safety needs; ensure that new data protection policies do not provide havens for criminals; standardize law enforcement requests for assistance to industry; allow industry to respond to incidents more quickly and with less expense; and develop 24-hour points of contact within critical ISPs. The subgroup is also working on a set of measures member countries can take to improve law enforcement's ability to locate and identify cyber criminals, including steps to address issues such as data preservation and retention, real-time tracing of communications, ISP cooperation with law enforcement, and user authentication.

The G-8's work has had several impacts. It has provided a model for activity by larger, formal multilateral efforts, including the Council of Europe's Convention on Cybercrime;[14] it has served to identify the key difficult issues that individual national governments and multilateral entities must resolve; and it has created a network that fosters both multilateral and bilateral informal cooperation on incident response. But ultimately, the *operational cooperative efforts are performed largely on a bilateral basis between the affected countries. In that sense, the G-8's principal accomplishment thus far has been to foster bilateral cooperation, not to replace it.*

So what type of informal, bilateral cooperation actually has occurred? The answer lies on two fronts: first, there has been extensive informal cooperation on investigations that cross national boundaries; and second, there has been informal cooperation in establishing mechanisms for sharing information and warnings about impending or ongoing attacks so that governments and companies can take protective steps before harm takes place.

INVESTIGATIONS

Bilateral cooperation on investigations has been going on for several years and has proven remarkably successful. To note a few examples involving the United States:

- In February and March 1998, hackers intruded into more than 500 military, civilian, government, and private-sector computer systems in the United States. The intrusions took place during the buildup of U.S. military personnel in the Middle East in response to tensions with Iraq over UN weapons inspections. The intruders penetrated at least 200 unclassified U.S. military and other government computer systems. The timing of the intrusions, and the fact that some activity appeared to come from an ISP in the Middle East, led many U.S. officials to suspect that this might be an instance of Iraqi information warfare. The U.S. National Infrastructure Protection Center (NIPC), an interagency entity located within the FBI, coordinated an extensive interagency investigation, code-named "Solar Sunrise." Internationally, the NIPC worked closely with Israeli law enforcement authorities. Within several days, the investigation determined that two teenagers in Cloverdale, California, and individuals in Israel were the true perpetrators.

- In February 2000, the NIPC received reports that CNN, Yahoo, Amazon.com, e-Bay, and other e-commerce sites had been subject to "Distributed Denial of Service" (DDOS) attacks, in which hackers intrude into and take over numerous networks and then use them to bombard the ultimate victim computer with bogus communications, thereby impeding the functionality of the victim network. The victim companies cooperated with the NIPC and several FBI offices in the United States and provided critical logs and other information. Within days, the FBI and NIPC had traced some of the attacks to Canada, and subsequently worked with the Royal Canadian Mounted Police (RCMP) to identify the suspect. The RCMP arrested a juvenile subject, who went by the name "Mafiaboy," in April 2000 for some of the attacks. Mafiaboy ultimately pleaded guilty to the attacks.

- Between January and March 2000, a hacker known as "Curador" victimized multiple e-commerce Web sites in the United States, Canada, Thailand, Japan, and the UK. Curador, whose real name was Raphael Gray, broke into the sites and stole as many as 28,000 credit card numbers, with losses estimated to be at least $3.5 million. Thousands of credit card numbers and expiration dates were posted to various Internet Web sites. After an extensive investigation, the FBI assisted the Dyfed Powys Police Service, a local Welsh police force, in a search at the residence of Mr. Gray. Mr. Gray was arrested and prosecuted in the UK under the UK's Computer Misuse Act of 1990. This case was predicated on the investigative work of the FBI, the Dyfed Powys Police, Internet security consultants, the RCMP, and the international banking and credit card industry.

- In May 2000, companies and individuals around the world were harmed by the "Love Bug" or "ILOVEYOU" virus (technically, a "worm"), which was propagated as an attachment to an e-mail message and spread rapidly through the address books of Microsoft Outlook users. Investigative work by the FBI, with assistance from the NIPC, traced the source of the virus to the Philippines within 24 hours. The FBI then worked with the Philippines' National Bureau of Investigation to identify the perpetrator, Onel de Guzman. The investigation in the Philippines was hampered by the lack of a specific computer-crime statute, and ultimately charges against Mr. de Guzman had to be dropped. Nevertheless, the speed with which the virus was traced back to its source was unprecedented. (The Philippine government later that year approved the E-Commerce Act, which now specifically criminalizes computer hacking and virus propagation.)

- Also in 2000, an individual gained unauthorized access to the internal computer system of Bloomberg, LP, a financial services company in New York, and stole sensitive information. That individual then e-mailed the CEO of Bloomberg, Michael Bloomberg (incidentally, the new mayor of New York City), and demanded that Bloomberg pay him $200,000 in exchange for providing information on how the hacker was able to infiltrate the system. With assistance from Mr. Bloomberg, the Metropolitan Police in London, and police in Almaty, Kazakhstan, the FBI was able to trace the intrusion back to Kazakhstan, identify two individuals involved, and lure the two individuals to a meeting in London, where the two were promptly arrested.

The success of these investigations is based in large part on the personal relationships, and resulting trust, that have developed between investigators from different countries. The FBI has been successful in developing these relationships in part because of the presence of FBI "Legal Attaches" (LEGATs) in over 40 countries around the world. The LEGATs allow the FBI to develop on-the-ground relationships with host-country investigators and to provide a liaison to expedite assistance between the United States and host country, in both directions.

In addition, the NIPC has provided cyber-crime investigation training to many of its international counterparts. This training serves not only to make foreign partners more capable of assisting in international investigations and of addressing cyber crime within their own borders, but also to establish personal relationships and trust among international investigators, which prove invaluable when an incident occurs and assistance is required. Much of this training takes place at the International Law Enforcement Academies in Budapest, Hungary, and Bangkok, Thailand. In addition, a small number of select international investigators receive training in NIPC-sponsored classes in the United States. The NIPC also holds workshops with other nations to share information on techniques and trends in cyber intrusions.[15]

WARNING

Given the speed with which destructive attacks can occur around the world (as demonstrated by the "Love Bug"), cooperation on investigations must be complemented by cooperation on sharing information to issue warnings, so that potential victims can take steps to protect themselves. To enhance such cooperation, the NIPC has established informal information-sharing relationships with watch centers in the UK, Canada, Australia, New Zealand, and Sweden. To further enhance such information sharing (which also assists in investigative cooperation), the UK, Canada, and Australia have seconded liaison representatives to the NIPC. The NIPC has also held discussions with several countries about how to establish their own NIPC-like entities, which would further enhance cooperation on warnings. Since the NIPC was founded in 1998, Japan, the UK, Canada, Germany, and Sweden have formed or are in the process of forming interagency entities like the NIPC.

CONCLUSION

In the absence of effective formal cooperation agreements, the United States and other countries have resorted to informal, bilateral cooperation as the principal means both of investigating international cyber-crime cases and of sharing information for the purpose of prevention and warning. These arrangements have succeeded in large part because of the trust that has been built up over time among the investigators in different countries. As Internet use spreads around the globe, however, cyber crime will occur in countries that have not traditionally been part of this trust network, testing the capacity of these informal arrangements. It is therefore imperative that more countries be brought into these informal arrangements as soon as possible, and also that they begin creating their own similar arrangements with like-minded states.

Inevitably, however, nations will find that a cyber attack has originated from or passed through a country that has not traditionally been an ally or a partner on law-enforcement matters. Cooperation on an investigation therefore will not be forthcoming. When this occurs, the informal bilateral cooperation model will have reached the limit of its effectiveness. It is therefore important that as countries expand the existing informal networks of bilateral and multilateral cooperation, they simultaneously begin to seek formal agreements that will commit all countries that are party to them to provide assistance to other parties. This will not be easy, but it is essential.

Notes

1. By cyber attacks, I mean computer-to-computer attacks to steal, erase, or alter information, or to destroy or impede the functionality of the victim computer system. These attacks typically fall into three general categories: (1) unauthorized intrusions, in which the attacker breaks into the computer system using various "hacking" techniques (or an "insider" exceeds his authorized access in order to do unauthorized things to the network); (2) destructive viruses or worms, which spread from computer to computer through e-mail or other forms of data exchange and can cause the loss of functionality of parts of the network; and (3) denial-of-service (DOS) attacks, in which the attacker may use several techniques to bombard the victim computer with different types of communications and essentially overload it, thereby impeding the victim computer's functionality.

2. CERT/CC saw nearly 10,000 incidents reported to it in 1999, 21,756 in 2000, and nearly 52,658 in 2001. See http://www.cert.org/stats/cert_stats.html.

3. See http://www.gocsi.com/prelea/000321.html. For instance, CSI found that 186 survey respondents reported $377,828,700 in financial losses in 2001, compared to 249 respondents reporting $265,589,940 in losses in 2000.

4. Computer Economics estimates that in 2001, the "ILOVEYOU" or "Love Bug" virus caused $8.75 billion in damage; in 2001, the SirCam attack caused $1.15 billion in damage, Code Red $2.62 billion, and Nimda $635 million; and in 1999, Melissa caused $1.10 billion in damage and Explorer $1.02 billion. See http://www.computereconomics.com/cei/press/pr92101.html.

5. Ibid.

6. This paper is limited to a discussion of "operational" cooperation—that is, cooperation among governmental entities charged with functional responsibility for handling incidents, which are typically law enforcement and security agencies. It does not address cooperation on policy development, research and development, or other important but nonoperational issues. Nor does it address intelligence or military cooperation.

7. As the U.S. Attorneys Manual, the guidebook for federal prosecutors in the United States, explains: "Most problems associated with international evidence gathering revolve around the concept of sovereignty. Virtually every nation vests responsibility for enforcing criminal laws in the sovereign. The other nation may regard an effort by an American investigator or prosecutor to investigate a crime or gather evidence within its borders as a violation of its sover-

eignty. Even such seemingly innocuous acts as a telephone call, a letter, or an unauthorized visit to a witness overseas may fall within this stricture. A violation of sovereignty can generate diplomatic protests and result in denial of access to the evidence or even the arrest of the agent or [prosecutor] who acts overseas. The solution is to invoke the aid of the foreign sovereign in obtaining the evidence." *U.S. Attorneys Manual,* Title 9-13.510, *Criminal Resource Manual* at 267. See http://www.usdoj.gov/usao/eousa/ foia_reading_room/usam/ title9/crm00267.htm.

8. In the absence of an MLAT, formal international arrangements might require prosecutors and investigators to rely on "letters rogatory" (or letters of request) to obtain evidence. Letters rogatory are essentially requests from one country's judiciary to another's to obtain and provide to the requesting country certain evidence or witness testimony. Obtaining the requisite court orders on each end of the request, pursuant to each country's different laws, can take considerable time. Indeed, the U.S. State Department warns that "[l]etters rogatory are a time consuming, cumbersome process and should not be utilized unless there are no other options available." See http://www.travel.state.gov/letters_rogatory.html.

9. See, for example, the Solar Sunrise case, discussed below. This case appeared at first to be a possible instance of information warfare, but turned out to involve hacking by teenagers in Israel and the United States. Compare this case with that of the Cuckoo's Egg in the 1980s, which appeared on its face to involve simple hacking to obtain free use of computers at the University of California at Berkeley, but turned out to involve intrusions into U.S. Defense Department computers by West German hackers who stole information and sold it to the Soviet KGB. See Clifford Stohl, *The Cuckoo's Egg: Tracking a Spy through the Maze of Computer Espionage* (New York: Doubleday, 1989).

10. In 1998, George Tenet, director of central intelligence, testified before the Senate Committee on Governmental Affairs that "we have identified several countries that have government-sponsored information warfare programs. Foreign nations have begun to include information warfare in their military doctrine as well as their war college curricula with respect to both offensive and defensive applications. It is clear that nations developing these programs recognize the value of attacking a country's computer systems—both on the battlefield and in the civilian arena." See http:// www.cia.gov/cia/public_affairs/speeches/archives/1998/dci_testimony_062498.html.

11. An intelligence agency from Country C, for example, could have routed its attack through Country B to cast suspicion on Country B. In another example, a destructive virus might be launched from a computer in Country B with damaging effects in several countries, including Country A. This could be the work of a military department in Country B. Or it could be the work of

teenage virus writers in Country B. Or it could be the work of teenage virus writers from Country A who intruded into the computer in Country B to make it more difficult to trace the true source of the virus. Or it could be the work of a military or intelligence agency from Country C doing the same thing and trying to cast suspicion on Country B. The possibilities for constructing a "hall of mirrors" in cyber space are almost endless.

12. The G-8 comprises the United States, the United Kingdom, France, Germany, Italy, Canada, Japan, and Russia.

13. The Subgroup on High-Tech Crime was formed under the auspices of the G-8's Senior Expert Group on Transnational Organized Crime, known as the "Lyon Group," because it first submitted a report to the heads of state at the G-8 summit in Lyon, France, in 1996. In December 1997, the G-8 justice and interior ministers met in Washington, D.C., and adopted 10 principles and a 10-point action plan to fight cyber crime. The G-8 heads of state endorsed the principles and action plan several months later, making this the first time that a multilateral group of heads of state agreed to a joint plan to fight cyber crime.

14. The Council of Europe (COE) is an international organization based in Strasbourg, France, with a pan-European membership of 41 countries. In 1989 and 1995, the COE adopted recommendations on computer-related crime that called on member states to consider computer crimes when either reviewing or proposing domestic legislation. These recommendations also contained principles on such topics as search and seizure, technical surveillance, electronic evidence, encryption, and international cooperation. In February 1997, a Committee of Experts on Crime in Cyberspace was formed to examine computer crime. Representatives from the United States attended as nonvoting observers. The committee developed a Cybercrime Convention that defines cyber-crime offenses and addresses such topics as jurisdiction, international cooperation, and search and seizure. The Cybercrime Convention was adopted by the council and is now being considered by member states for implementation through national legislation.

15. For example, in September 1999 the NIPC sponsored an International Cyber Crime Conference in New Orleans, Louisiana, to provide training to international law-enforcement officers and forge links between foreign law-enforcement officers and personnel representing numerous U.S. law-enforcement agencies.

CHAPTER TWO

A GATE MUST EITHER BE OPEN OR BE SHUT

THE COUNCIL OF EUROPE CYBERCRIME
CONVENTION MODEL

Henrik Kaspersen

The title of this chapter was taken from a play written by Alfred de Musset (1810–1857). It shows that the dilemma in balancing friendliness and security is not new. With regard to fighting cyber crime, as with any type of crime, prevention and repression should go hand in hand. This essay will concentrate on the Cybercrime Convention (CCC) as an important vehicle for treaty-based international cooperation in this field, but it will also demonstrate the need for particular flanking measures.

THE IT ENVIRONMENT

Historians looking back on the twentieth century will express amazement at the societal changes in the industrialized areas of our planet, caused mainly by the emergence, during a relatively short period of less than 50 years, of information technology (IT). IT has dramatically changed the ways and methods of industrial production; it has strongly enhanced the development of services as an important part of national incomes; it has strongly influenced the organization of society and private organizations; and, in particular, it has led to strong globalization of economic and other activities. Remarkably, one of the facilities that contributed significantly to these developments, the Internet, became a mass medium for communication only after 1995. Unlike many articles on the topic, I will not start with the usual ARPANET references but restrict myself to the conclusion that the Internet is a precious commodity for our economies and for social life. It would be hard to think about a world without it. Because of the way it emerged it has a kind of democratic structure. Hardware, software, or content providers do not dominate it. It is a (market) place, where organizations as well as individual persons are engaged in the offering, rendering, and consumption of all kinds of services, economically relevant or not. The statistics of users of the Internet are adequate proof of its raison d'être.[1]

From the viewpoint of a democratic society, the Internet is an important means for citizens to execute their democratic rights, such as freedom of expression and the right to gather and exchange information. The Internet already has an important meaning in society as an independent source of information compared to existing mass media. Because of technical developments and because of the demands of their citizens, governments of democratic states will be forced to use the Internet more and more in order to improve the participation of citizens in the functioning of the institutions of democratic society. From the viewpoint of economic development, the Internet provides important opportunities for economic activity—as a marketplace where buyers and sellers can meet and do business. From the viewpoint of education and science, the Internet enables the sharing of information and views at a global level, thus stimulating international debate and further elaboration of the results of such debate.

The end of these developments cannot yet be seen. The first steps to broadband communications, enabling full communication of multimedia information, have just been taken. Large investments will have to be made in order to provide the average Internet user with adequate communication facilities.

The Internet's connecting of millions of computer systems and thus millions of people has also a dark side. Where so many people can be reached by means of simple procedures and little effort, there will be always be people who will try to misuse such communication facilities for criminal purposes. The more the Internet is used for all kinds of communications and business transactions, the wider the circle of persons that will misuse it to commit crimes or misuse its facilities for criminal purposes.

THE ANSWER: INTERNATIONAL COOPERATION?

Crimes on the Internet occur in an international, global environment. Criminals, victims, and intermediaries find themselves in different physical locations with different cultural, social, economics, and legal orders. It has been argued that the Internet or its successor will eventually, like in a system of communicating vessels, diffuse the different national orders into a single world order. This may be a realistic prospect, but it will not happen by itself and not within the short term. With regard to combating of cyber crime, the usual call of the public and of politicians is for criminal law solutions. In this respect I would like to emphasize that criminal law should be the last resort—that is, criminal law should only be invoked where other solutions, including other legal means as embodied in civil and administrative law, will fail or are impracticable.

Having said that does not mean that the criminal law system, as such, is not capable of dealing with obnoxious conduct. Substantive criminal law should set behavioral standards in the first place, and procedural criminal law should provide the authority and means to perform any criminal investigation. Development of technology will bring the need for permanent review of the powers of criminal procedural laws in order to ensure that criminal investigations remain possible. Consider, for example, the analysis of blood and DNA samples or X-ray tests to investigate the smuggling of drugs. Information technology and its applications create a parallel need for investigation in computer systems and networks. To that end, I will discuss the history and background of the Cybercrime Convention (hereafter CCC) and explain what the convention means for international cooperation. According to the schedule for this conference, it is my task to deal with formal treaty-based international cooperation. In the text hereafter I will demonstrate that such formal cooperation cannot do without forms of informal cooperation, both bilateral and multilateral.

THE CYBERCRIME CONVENTION

Parties of the Convention

After a process of four years of negotiation (who said that legislators work fast!), 30 parties signed the Cybercrime Convention in Budapest on November 23, 2001.[2] This is a high percentage of the 47 countries that were entitled to sign and a precedent in the Council of Europe practice of treaty making. Because a relatively low number of ratifications (5) is necessary to bring the convention into force, it may be expected that this will happen within one and a half to two years. The United States, Canada, Japan, and South Africa signed the convention also, as non-European states. As a consequence, the convention has already been signed by all the member states of the G-8 and by all the member states of the European Union. Member states of the Council of Europe are entitled to enter the convention at any time and are supposed to do so in the short term. Other new parties can only access the convention when it has come into force and if the ratifying parties approve to accept the new party under the rules of the Council of Europe.

Aim of the Convention

The purpose of the convention is threefold. Within the scope of the convention, it aims at the harmonization of criminal law (i.e., the harmonization of substantive criminal law concerning conduct that qualifies as cyber crime). Such harmonization is necessary in order to prevent some territories from becoming "data havens," where cyber criminals would enjoy the protection of local law while being subject to criminal investigations and prosecutions in other states. What has to be considered as cyber crime will be discussed later in the section on substantive law provisions.

A second goal is the harmonization of criminal procedural law concerning criminal investigations in public and private computer systems and networks. The volatility of computer data requires special powers and measures for law enforcement authorities. It should be ensured that the parties to the CCC are able to perform criminal investigations in computer networks and computer systems in the first place, in order to prevent a situation in which cyber criminals under the jurisdiction of one party would know that they are beyond the reach of other national law enforcement authorities. These powers and measures will be dealt with later in the section on jurisdictional provisions.

The third aim of the convention is to facilitate mutual legal assistance between the parties of the CCC in the investigation and prosecution of cyber crime. In the CCC, but also in other international instruments, the principle of dual criminality is an important precondition for international cooperation (e.g., in the form of extradition or mutual legal assistance). In principle, there is no obligation to render mutual legal assistance when the requested party does not criminalize the underlying conduct. For instance, in the multilateral Council of Europe Convention on Mutual Legal Assistance of 1959, the principal rule was that parties would provide for legal assistance even where there was no dual criminality. That convention, however, allowed parties to reserve the right to raise the condition of dual criminality, which a large number did.[3] Dual criminality, therefore, plays an important role in mutual assistance in criminal matters.

The fourth aim is to codify international public law. International communication networks cross national borders. A principal question is how territory-based jurisdictional rules can be applied to territory-independent communications and data flowing through international computer and telecommunication networks. Therefore, the CCC precisely stipulates a limited number of cases in which law enforcement is entitled to engage in transborder investigations. The general rule of international public law, however (also reflected in the convention), is that in cases where evidence or other material must be obtained from another state, states should refrain from interfering with persons, goods, and computer data within the territory of another state and that the instruments of mutual assistance should be followed. Mutual legal assistance will be dealt with later in the section on procedural law provisions.

The fifth aim of the CCC is to provide for an international legal framework to enable further development and common understanding of the important issues noted above. The CCC obliges its parties to review the instruments of the CCC on a regular basis and provides for a flexible and timely amendment procedure for the adoption of specific protocols. This procedure is described below.

Scope of the Convention

The convention has a minimum character. According to the Vienna Convention on the Law of Treaties,[4] parties are always entitled to go further in their national law than agreed in the international instrument, provided that such measures are not contradictory to the instrument concerned. The CCC seeks to provide a minimum basis for international cooperation.

For this reason the CCC contains a number of substantive criminal provisions and relating regulation. The substantive part of the convention deals with so-called cyber crimes, specific types of crime for which the parties are obliged to assure that such conduct is punishable under their domestic law. This part of the convention is partly an elaboration of the Council of Europe Recommendation of 1989.[5] The latter instrument had not led sufficiently to the intended harmonization of national criminal legislation concerning computer-related crime. As part of a binding international instrument the impetus to national legislators will be much stronger. Of course, new elements and new crimes were added, as will be discussed later.

The procedural powers under the CCC are specific powers to investigate cyber crime. Significantly, where substantive law has a restricted meaning, in relation to the procedure, cyber crime is defined as any conduct as specified in the substantive law—but also any crime the investigation of which requires data to be selected, gathered, and secured from computer systems and networks. In principle, the convention could apply to any crime as long as the clues that lead to the perpetrator and (other) possible evidence can be found with a computer system or network.

Further, the convention deals with mutual legal assistance between its parties. It defines the relation between existing instruments for mutual assistance between parties and the instruments of the convention. If no other legal instrument is available the convention provides a comprehensive minimum set of rules for cooperation.

Substantive Law Provisions

Under the heading of cyber crime, the convention defines a number of crimes that are categorized as follows. Criminal behavior directed against computer systems and their data content is indicated by the term "CIA offenses" (crimes against the confidentiality, integrity, and availability of computer systems, their processing capacity, or their data content). Most of the offenses were part of the Recommendation of the Council of Europe from 1989, such as illegal access to a computer system, illegal data interference, and system interference. In the CCC these provisions have been modernized and extended. Provisions regarding the criminalization of the production, distribution, and possession of hardware and software tools, including passwords, for the purpose of committing one of these crimes are new.

A second category is computer-related crime, consisting of computer-related fraud and computer-related forgery. The aim of these two provisions is to ensure that the parties to the convention do not differentiate in their national criminal law concerning the applicability of relevant provisions as to whether a fraud or a forgery is committed in relation to or by means of IT. Under these provisions fraud with and forgery of electronic means of payment shall be criminalized.

A third category concerns the criminalization of violations of copyright and related rights. The provision follows the TRIPS agreement (trade-related aspects of international property rights) and obliges the criminalization of conduct that is "on an economic scale." The provision extends this obligation to neighboring rights and the forthcoming World Intellectual Property Organization (WIPO) treaties.

A fourth category is indicated as content-related crimes. The one example so far in the treaty concerns the production, offering, dissemination, possession, and procurement of electronic child pornography. Most of the parties to the convention have child pornography provisions in their national criminal codes. This provision, although restricted to the electronic environment, will bring a strong harmonization because parties will not differentiate between the tangible and the electronic environment. Negotiating parties could not agree on a second content-related provision: the production, offering, and dissemination of electronic racist and xenophobic material. Some parties, like the United States, are not in a position to implement such a provision because constitutional freedom of speech stands in the way. For that reason a separate protocol to the convention is at present being negotiated in Strasbourg.

In the latter category the framework nature of the convention is best demonstrated. Parties could in the future agree to bring harmonized content-related crimes under the scope of the convention, such as the illegal offering of gambling or the illegal offering of products and services.

Jurisdiction Provisions

The jurisdiction part (Article 22) is related to the application of criminal offenses of the CCC. Under their national systems the courts will usually give a broad interpretation of *locus delicti* (e.g., the crime is considered to have been committed within the territory of the state if the victim was residing there, even if the perpetrator acted from another territory). In international computer networks this situation will be the rule rather than the exception. As a consequence, more than one state may claim jurisdiction over conduct in international networks. The chapter contains rules to determine the most appropriate jurisdiction. Parties are also obliged to establish jurisdiction over cyber crimes committed by their nationals if they commit a crime in another territory, provided that the law of that territory has criminalized such conduct; or when no state has territorial jurisdiction over such crimes.

Procedural Law Provisions

The investigative powers under Chapter II of the CCC concern the following. A distinction is made between data stored in a computer system and data flowing within or between computer systems. This distinction, maintained in most domestic systems, is retained because of the different procedures and safeguards for the persons concerned.

- Powers related to the investigation and gathering of data from computer systems and networks (search and seizure, Article 19). These powers include accessory powers such as the power to order the assistance of persons not under suspicion in order to access a system or its content.

- Powers related to the real-time collection of traffic data concerning electronic communications (Article 19). The CCC provides for two alternatives: law enforcement authorities may do it themselves or they may order the telecom operator or Internet service provider (ISP) to do it for them. Although the CCC does not oblige ISPs to take technical measures in order to ensure applicability of the measure, parties to the convention may take such legal measures in their national law. "Traffic data" in the meaning of the CCC is data about certain communications by which the source of the communication can be established (Article 1d).

- Powers related to the real-time interception of electronic communications (Article 20). The provision is drafted in parallel to Article 19. The scope of application for both powers is serious crimes only, to be further determined by national law.

- Powers to order the production of certain electronic data in possession of or under control of certain persons under the jurisdiction of a party (Article 18).

- Powers to order the expedited preservation of volatile computer data (Article 16). An equivalent separate power is given concerning traffic data (Article 17). The powers of Article 18 are used to bring the data under control of law enforcement.

It should be noted that the CCC leaves the provision of safeguards concerning the application of its coercive powers largely to domestic law. The reason for this is these safeguards already exist in national criminal procedural law. The principles of such safeguards are in general the same but the modalities and conditions differ considerably. Harmonization of such safeguards, if possible at all, was far beyond the task and the possibilities of the drafting committee. The member states of the Council of Europe will, in any case, be subject to judicial control by the European Court of Human Rights in Strasbourg. Parties to the convention that are not signatories to the Rome Convention have incorporated in their laws similar principles and avail over equivalent means of judicial control. Moreover, according to the rules of accession, new parties to the convention that do not provide for such safeguards cannot be accepted.

Mutual Legal Assistance (MLA)

General Principles

Article 23 states that mutual assistance should be rendered "to the widest extent possible." This principle invites the parties to minimize potential impediments and to speed up procedures where possible. Further, in case of capacity problems, mutual assistance should not automatically be given the lowest priority. The meaning of this article is not that parties render assistance in violation of their national law.

Article 23 further defines the scope of the obligation to cooperate under the CCC. Unless ruled otherwise, mutual assistance should be rendered concerning the crimes defined by the CCC as well as any other crime for the investigation of which data have to secured from computer systems or networks, as defined in Article 14.

Article 23 also determines the relation of the CCC to existing instruments of mutual assistance that are in force between the parties involved in the request for and rendering of mutual assistance. The CCC does not supersede the existing arrangements but has a supplemental nature, thus expanding the scope of international cooperation. This flexible system allows the application of the most appropriate legal rule in favor of international cooperation.

The specific provisions of the CCC concerning extradition add the crimes defined in the substantive part of the convention to the list of extraditable offences in the relevant international instruments that are in force between the parties to the CCC. The CCC refers to possible minimum thresholds in those instruments and applies those in the CCC.

Article 24 deals with extradition of suspects of cyber crimes in the meaning of the substantive law provisions of the CCC. The parties should consider a number of the offenses defined by the CCC as extraditable offences. The relevant provisions in the CCC are meant to supplement the existing arrangements between parties to the convention.

Article 25 reiterates some principles applying to mutual legal assistance. It stresses that a party must have a legal base in its national law to render the requested assistance. It also provides for the use of modern communication technologies as means to request mutual assistance and avoids a too-narrow interpretation of the term "dual criminality."

Article 26 provides for the spontaneous provision of information to law enforcement authorities of another party without prior request (e.g., when evidence has been obtained about a crime that may involve another party).

The point and spirit of these articles is to achieve an international cooperation that time-consuming formal requirements do not hamper, to ensure that the rules concerning cooperation are interpreted in a way favorable to that cooperation and that the parties concerned may provide assistance to each other without formal requests.

Relation to Other MLA Instruments

The general idea under the CCC is that if a requested party is authorized to give assistance, it should do so, either under existing bilateral or multilateral MLA treaties or on the basis of the CCC. The CCC therefore supplements the existing instruments. If no legal basis in other instruments can be found, the CCC provides in Articles 27 and 28 for a minimum set of provisions to enable mutual assistance. The thrust of the CCC, again, is to remove possible hurdles and create adequate opportunities for international cooperation.

Measures of MLA

Parties may request the execution of certain powers in the requested state. These precise powers have been discussed in the domestic part. In addition, a party under the CCC is obliged to have an operational

24-hours-a-day/7-days-a-week contact point in order to ensure that a request for assistance can be expeditiously executed (e.g., that such a request can be forwarded immediately to the appropriate office, which will have all the necessary information to proceed).

Preference for Mutual Assistance

The question of if and how states could establish jurisdiction over the whole or a part of global communication infrastructures like the Internet was debated thoroughly in the CCC drafting process. Usually, jurisdiction is related but also restricted to the territory of an individual state. In particular cases, states are recognized to also have jurisdiction over their ships and aircrafts. Courts will also claim jurisdiction over certain crimes on the basis of an extensive interpretation of *locus delicti*. According to international law, the execution of powers by law enforcement authorities should not be extended beyond the limits of the national territory, except for the cases referred to below. IT enables persons, including law enforcement authorities, to give effect to their acts in a location other than where they actually reside. After ample debate, it was concluded that, for reasons of principle and practice, parties to the CCC should not undertake investigative measures against computer systems and their content if such systems were not physically present within the territorial competences of such states. In those cases, the path of mutual legal assistance should be followed. In a few cases, the convention allows transborder activity. Article 32 gives two examples under CCC where transborder investigative activities are not considered to be a violation of international law. In the case of publicly accessible databases or Web sites, law enforcement agents of another party are entitled to access and download this information. The second case allows that law enforcement agents may investigate data located in the territory in another party if the competent person in their jurisdiction authorizes them. In addition, Article 18 provides that a person present in the territory of another state can be ordered to submit certain data from a computer system—also in cases where a system is located in the territory of another party. The flexible and expedited means for mutual assistance, as provided by the CCC, should be a guarantee that the requested assistance can be given without delay and without retarding formalities in the procedure.

Final Provisions

Final provisions involve most of the usual topics, dealing with declarations and reservations, terms of the convention coming into force, and terms of accession by other parties. One exceptional provision should be mentioned here. The drafters of the convention were very concerned that its content would not guard against rapid developments of information technology and the emergence of new applications, including the misuse of those applications. For that reason, the CCC contains an obligation for the parties to consult on a regular basis about the implementation and practical experiences with the convention, in view of possible amendments to it. The amendment procedure itself is flexible and can be realized in relatively short term.

Meaning and Impact of the Convention

The obligations under the CCC, as is the case of most international conventions, have a minimum character. When implementing the content of the CCC in their domestic law, the parties may go beyond it (e.g., may criminalize conduct that is not included in the convention) or provide for legal powers that are more far reaching than provided for in the convention, unless this would contravene the content and the spirit of the convention. Concerning substantive law requirements, harmonization may extend to traditional crimes, about which the convention deals as "electronic modalities." Parties may not implement exemptions as given in the provisions of the CCC if not necessary for national purposes. It was already noted that some countries, which do not even envision joining the convention, apply its substantive part as a model law and implement it in their domestic law on a voluntary basis.

What has been said about the substantive criminal law is also valid for the procedural part. Parties to the convention will apply the principles of some investigative legal tools concerning computer systems and networks to other investigative powers as well. Here the parties will profit from the innovative nature of the convention. Of course, other countries will also consider the procedural content of the convention as a model law and copy it into their domestic law.

EVALUATION

Mutual legal assistance is a highly formalized system of international cooperation. Because criminal investigations (usually) interfere with fundamental rights of the defendant and other persons concerned, the powers of law enforcement authorities should be defined precisely, and the law should provide for adequate safeguards in particular for the people who are the object of the execution of such powers. The requirement of formalities, slow and careful proceedings, and a minimum of flexibility make that clear. At certain points the CCC breaks out of the present regime of mutual legal assistance by the introduction of preliminary measures that should be carried out expeditiously without the possibility to check if the usual formal requirements for a regular request for assistance have been met.

It should be noted that mutual legal assistance as such does not imply an obligation to cooperate in the broadest sense (e.g., by taking common measures to combat cyber crime). The decision to investigate and prosecute a cyber crime is at the discretion of the law enforcement authorities of the national state, if national law so determines. If in the course of an investigation the assistance of another Party is sought—to arrest a suspect or to obtain evidence, for example—instruments of mutual assistance can be applied so that a contracting party is obliged to render such assistance, within the scope of the CCC and other MLA instruments and in as far as its national law allows it.

It should be stressed in particular that the final provisions of the CCC further enhance international cooperation on a structural basis, because parties have undertaken to review and amend the convention in close concert. This cooperation does not only involve mutual legal assistance but also the activities of law enforcement authorities in the parties concerned.

The global nature of the Internet requires closer cooperation of law enforcement authorities at all levels. These authorities will not only exchange information about individual cases as permitted by their laws, but also exchange experience and knowledge about investigative techniques and tools. For example, as part of the regular G-8 meetings, law enforcement authorities, on the basis of the 1997 Action Plan, work together and exchange experiences, technical knowledge, and information about software tools developed for the investigation of cyber crime.[6] Also, for the countries that do not participate in the work of the G-8, training and obtaining technical expertise is imperative. Within the Interpol organization some common projects or working groups have been established.[7] Most of the international cooperation still seems to occur through the informal old-boys network. One could imagine that formalized forms of cooperation would be preferred.

Victims may be expected to report cyber crimes to the responsible authorities. However, it has long been known that a fraction of such crimes are reported to the police. This may have many reasons, of which the most important is that victims do not have high expectations that the perpetrator will be found and prosecuted. In addition, victims would rather accept the damage done than get involved in a police investigation. Of course this may differ if the crime is more serious. A solution, but a bad one, could be that a person (except the suspect) who has knowledge of a cyber crime is under a legal obligation to report such a crime to the authorities. This approach is known in several legislatures, in particular in relation to very serious crimes. The enforcement of a provision that would criminalize the nonreporting of cyber crimes is in practice hardly possible and therefore should not be done. The reporting of cyber crimes to the police should be enhanced but other instruments should have preference. For instance, in some countries watchdog groups surf the Internet and look for particular content-related crimes, such as the distribution of child pornography or hate speech. These watchdog groups may inform the ISP that is hosting the contested material and leave action toward the subscriber to the that provider. The ISP may demand that the subscriber remove the material or the provider may remove the material itself, as authorized by the subscriber agreement.

Informed ISPs are under a (civil) obligation to act in order to prevent their liability. If the provider or the subscriber fails to remove the material, the watchdog group hands the dossier over to the police. In the field of intellectual property rights, collective rights organizations and interest groups may take action against infringements, including reporting cases to law enforcement. Of course, for such watchdog groups and others, coordination and cooperation with law enforcement authorities is necessary. Law enforcement authorities also could give guidance to judge what is illegal and what is not. Governments should enhance the establishment of such watchdog groups and enhance international cooperation between them.[8]

A last but extremely important point is the awareness of Internet users of the risks of becoming victims of cyber crime. The single global infrastructure, the standardization of communication software, and the low level of professionalism of the average user make them extremely vulnerable to crime. The average Internet user has a highly unjustified confidence in the reliability and the safety of the Internet and potentially is a willing victim for an experienced and skilled but criminal partner in communication. Therefore, governments should take both national and international initiatives to mobilize users. Users should be made more aware of the risks they run and the risks to which they place others by not taking appropriate security measures. Because these risks do not differ from country to country, an internationally coordinated approach could be more effective.

FINAL OBSERVATION

The CCC was drafted for the purpose of mutual legal assistance. It has a number of important related effects to the national legislation of the parties concerned that improve the possibilities of combating cyber crime. In the previous paragraph it has been argued that the CCC should have its place amid other kinds of initiatives in international cooperation, both formal and informal, to shape an effective approach to the prevention and repression of cyber crimes.

Notes

1. Worldwide, more than 500 million people are online. See http://www.nua.ie/surveys/ how_many_online and http://glreach.com/globstats/index.php3.

2. Convention ETS 185 of November 23, 2001.

3. Convention ETS 30 of April 20, 1959. In particular, Article 5.

4. May 23, 1969, in force January 27, 1980 (UN Document A/Conference 39/28, UKTS 58 [1980], 8 ILM 679).

5. R (1989) 9.

6. For general information, see the G8 Information Centre, http://www.g7.utoronto.ca.

7. Working Parties on Information Technology Crimes in America, Europe, and Asia. See, for example, http://www.interpol.int/Public/Technology Crime/default.asp.

8. Apart from what already has been achieved. See, for example, http://www.inhope.org with member organizations in Germany, the UK, France, the Netherlands, Belgium, Norway, and the United States.

CHAPTER THREE

LAYING THE FOUNDATIONS FOR A CYBER-SECURE WORLD
Pottengal Mukundan

ASSESSING THE PROBLEM

To formulate a worthwhile strategy to combat any crime, it is first necessary to obtain accurate information on the methods, frequency, and target of the crime in question so that resources, whether in terms of manpower or finance, can be allocated effectively.

In the case of computer-related crime, or, as it is commonly known, cyber crime, there is a pressing need for specific data, on not only the modus operandi of the attack and the victim, but also the geographical location of the perpetrator(s) and the target.

There have been many blanket statistics given concerning the worldwide harm caused by particular strains of computer viruses/ worms. For example the Love Bug virus, which struck in May 2000, is said to have caused an estimated U.S. $10 billion of damage globally. More detailed and focused information covering the whole spectrum of cyber crime has been published in the form of surveys, most notably by the Computer Security Institute and the San Francisco FBI's Computer Intrusion Squad in the form of an annual survey.

Although such surveys provide invaluable information, they tend to provide a country-specific snapshot rather than a global picture of cyber crime. By their very nature, surveys are to a large extent historic. By analyzing surveys over a number of years or by drawing on the conclusions of the latest survey, trends can be predicted. However, there will always be a time lag between the emergence of a new threat and its inclusion in a survey.

Overcoming the delay factor is especially crucial when it comes to cyber crime. For example, the Love Bug virus took five hours to reach its peak. In part what is needed, therefore, is a constant flow of information to provide a proactive, as opposed to reactive, response. For example, by the time many software patches to fix security flaws or new antivirus signatures are made available, much of the damage has already been done. This is in no way a criticism of computer security companies; it is merely a statement of fact.

AN OVERVIEW OF THREATS

The criminal fraternity is becoming increasingly attracted to Internet crime because of the anonymity it offers. Robbing a bank through a remote computer is a lot less risky than donning a mask and waving a shotgun and can be far more profitable. The 1994 Citibank fraud provides a prime example of just how much money can be moved electronically by criminal means. A Russian hacker believed to be acting at the behest of the Russian mafia siphoned off more than $10 million.

The Internet is also vulnerable to acts of wanton vandalism. Distributed Denial of Service (DDOS) attacks have continued to generate much concern. Briefly, a DDOS attack is where Web servers, routers, and other network devices are subject to a flood of traffic so that the network is unavailable to legitimate users. This kind of attack immobilized the likes of CNN, Yahoo, eBay, and Amazon in February 2000. Worrisomely, software can be easily downloaded to automate such attacks, which brings the attacks within the capabilities of the fairly low-skilled hacker, or script kiddies as they are often called.

New viruses continue to be unleashed across a greater number of platforms. Last year saw the goner worm infect computers around the world. Experts have described that worm as a "blended threat" in that it combines the computer-crashing properties of worms with code that attempts to gain control of infected computers so that they can be controlled remotely, typically to launch DDOS attacks.

In the third quarter of 2001, Belgium called for a global early warning system for computer viruses. Following the outbreak of the

Love Bug virus, Belgium set up its own early warning center, which it has said has dramatically reduced the damage caused by viruses to smaller companies that cannot afford a permanent information technology (IT) security personnel presence.

As society becomes ever more dependent on the Internet and communication networks, the likelihood of damage in human rather than just financial terms becomes a real possibility. A number of critical services depend on computers, including ambulance, fire, and traffic control.

New threats will continue to emerge as technology advances apace. For example, as more organizations switch to wireless networks the threat grows of hackers literarily plucking data out of thin air, armed only with a laptop and a cheap wireless card, using the equipment to eavesdrop on information being broadcast.

WINNING THE TRUST OF BUSINESS

Businesses are generally reluctant to report instances of cyber crime because of the fear that the harm caused by a falloff in consumer/client confidence will be greater than any direct loss suffered. The perception is that the target is not purely viewed as a victim but is also seen by the public as in some way culpable for the attack. Although a business that fails to take adequate security measures may be construed as being negligent, guarding against all possible forms of attack is not possible. With respect to DDOS attacks, as Internet security is highly interdependent, a system remains vulnerable regardless of how well defended it is. The ultimate state of security rests on other users of the Internet.

With DDOS attacks, because the Web site will be down and no legitimate traffic can get through, knowledge that a particular company has been attacked will soon be public. The same is also true for Web defacements. In theory, companies should be more forthcoming about reporting such incidents. Where a company has its servers hacked into with the possible compromise of confidential information, however, they are less likely to be willing to report the attack immediately.

It should be stressed, though, that the reporting of an incident is not the same as making it public. Setting up a confidential reporting center to forward information to regulatory authorities and law enforcement, and provide advance warnings to business of threats on the horizon, could help overcome the disinclination of companies to report an attack. Businesses should be encouraged to report incidents not just for altruistic reasons but because it will benefit them in the long term by giving them access to vital intelligence to help avoid future attacks and losses.

To make the best use of the data obtained on attacks and let those providing the information see that it is being put to good use, a suitable framework to facilitate international cooperation should be established.

THE CONVENTION APPROACH

In bringing the perpetrators of crime to justice, problems of jurisdiction obviously arise where the crime is committed in one country by someone residing in another country. Although this can be a factor in other types of crime, it is most keenly felt in cyber crime because of the borderless nature of this type of crime.

In order for a country to bring criminal charges against a person, that country must be able to exercise jurisdiction over the individual in question. The U.S. Constitution, for example, permits U.S. courts to exercise personal jurisdiction over any person who has what is deemed to be sufficient minimum contact with the United States. Other problems remain, however, such as extradition and competing national laws.

Within a formal framework, the cooperation between two countries through a mutual treaty is a quicker and less complicated process than one encompassing many nations. Should the attack originate elsewhere, however, the treaty is of little use. The most recent and well-publicized example of a transnational treaty designed for the purpose of the adoption of appropriate legislation and the fostering of international cooperation with respect to cyber crime is the Council of Europe's Convention on Cybercrime.

Two problems exist with the sole reliance on multinational conventions. The first is the time element. The Cybercrime Convention, for example, underwent numerous draft revisions before 30 countries signed it in November 2001, and it still requires 5 countries to ratify it by incorporating it into their legislation before it comes into force. Second, the problem of the originator of the crime residing in a country that is not a member of the appropriate convention remains. To make matters worse, the act perpetrated may not be a crime in the country in which it originated.

The culprit behind the Love Bug virus, a Filipino, could only be charged with crimes carrying relatively light sentences because the Philippines did not have laws at that time that specifically outlawed the dissemination of computer viruses. This loophole has since been closed, but an important role may exist for a transnational cyber-crime prevention body to advise other countries of omissions in their laws that allow acts of cyber crime to go unpunished. Such advice has the advantage of not being dependent on any convention.

In 2000, a report on cyber crime and punishment by a technology management consulting firm found that only 9 of the 52 countries surveyed had amended their laws to deal with at least 6 of the 10 types of offenses listed. The offenses fell into four categories: data-related crimes covering interception, modification, and theft; network-related crimes covering interference and sabotage; crimes and access covering hacking and virus distribution; and associated computer-related crimes covering aiding and abetting computer criminals, computer fraud, and computer forgery. Another 10 countries had some form of legislation against cyber crime, but 33 countries had no law against computer crime at all (although 17 of those were in the process of updating their legislation).

There are precedents in other areas of international crime that deal with the jurisdictional issue. One of these is the UN Convention on the Suppression of Unlawful Acts against the Safety of Maritime Navigation (the SUA or Rome convention of 1988). This convention arose from the hijacking of a cruise vessel in the Mediterranean. The vessel was registered in Liberia, the owners were Italian, the hijackers were from the Middle East, the crew were of different nationalities, the passengers (one of whom was killed) were from the United States, and the attack took place on high seas. The issue was who had the right to investigate and prosecute the offenders. Article 10 of the SUA Convention obliges the coastal state in which the offenders are found to try them under their own laws if they do not extradite them to the flag state.

THE BENEFITS OF INFORMAL FRAMEWORKS

A strategy not based around a treaty has the advantage of being able to respond in a speedier and more flexible manner, which is important, considering the fast evolving patterns and developments in cyber crime. A nontreaty approach may also be seen as more friendly and less "big brother" by legitimate businesses, which voiced such criticisms about the Cybercrime Convention, despite its good intentions. An informal approach based on a central forum can also help pave the way for the acceptance of a convention among the business community by acting as the representative of business and raising any concerns with government. It is also easier and less time-consuming for government to deal with one organization rather than numerous trade bodies or a multitude of companies.

TRADITIONAL AND NEW CRIME

Not only business needs a flow of constant, accurate, and speedy information to alert it to any incoming threat. Information is important to focus and shape opinion and action by both business and government.

Budgetary constraints often mean that law enforcement is underfunded and lacks adequate manpower and training. A savvy criminal may take advantage of this by choosing to carry out a traditional crime through computer-related means to slow down the investigation process or avoid detection altogether. It is therefore important to establish whether such a shift is occurring so that resources can be better allocated. Investigations into cyber crime might also be carried out by specialist cyber-crime units as well as by the law enforcement departments responsible for traditional crimes.

Cyber crime crosses not only geographical boundaries but also fields of expertise. This is reflected by the comments of a senior British police officer who in 2000 said that the types of crimes committed in cyber space now closely mirror offenses committed in the "real world." Fraud, drug dealing, pedophilia, organized crime, terrorism, cyber stalking, and civil disturbance have now joined the established forms of Internet crime such as computer hacking and the propagation of computer viruses.

Businesses may find themselves a victim of cyber crime either as a blind target, for example, through a virus spread globally and indiscriminately, or as a specific target through financial fraud or hacking. In the wider picture, business will rely on law enforcement to perform a general crime prevention role, for example, the identification and prosecution of the authors of a particular virus/worm.

Businesses face two problems when they become the sole target of a cyber crime. The police may not have the requisite skills or manpower, and a company may be reluctant to be part of a public prosecution for fear of negative publicity.

THE IMB PIRACY MODEL

Given the slender and overstretched resources of law enforcement in many parts of the world, business has a vital role to play in providing much-needed support and information to law enforcement, government, and the business community. The International Maritime Bureau (IMB) piracy model has been a remarkable example of a successful attempt to harness the forces of law enforcement agencies, governments, and business to bring international piracy under control.

In 1991 ship-operating members of the IMB complained that attacks against their vessels in certain parts of Asia were increasing and that they were receiving little or no support from law enforcement agencies. Inquiries by the IMB to law enforcement agencies indicated that the IMB and the agencies were not being notified of the cases of piracy. The common complaint of the agencies was that ship operators were not cooperating to enable the offenders to be brought to trial. In some cases, certain law enforcement agencies also found it convenient to avoid dealing with these attacks by claiming that they had no jurisdiction.

The conflict was a classic example of the priorities of business versus law enforcement. Ship owners wanted the problem to be dealt with by law enforcement, but they were not prepared to accept the commercial consequences of having their vessels delayed in port while law enforcement officers took statements and collected evidence. In many cases, victimized crew members were not prepared to go to court in the country of attack to give evidence against the pirates. Law enforcement sometimes saw this international crime as draining its resources, with little direct relevance to the public to which it was accountable (i.e., the victims, crew members, ship owners, cargo owners, and their underwriters were foreign interests). The crimes in many cases took place beyond the immediate horizon of the national press and public. The costs of investigating and prosecuting these crimes were, in some cases, seen to be disproportionate to the impact they had on local society. Law enforcement was also not prepared to concede that the commercial interests of the ship owners took priority over their need to collect the evidence that would ensure successful prosecution.

The IMB set up its Piracy Reporting Center in Kuala Lumpur, funded by business. It began to collect data on the attacks of piracy. It found that shipping interests were more prepared to report to a business-sponsored reporting center than to law enforcement. These reports were promptly passed on to law enforcement agencies for their action. The daily reports were compiled into quarterly reports, which were compiled into annual reports. The quarterly and annual reports contained considerable detail on the attacks. This information proved to be vital to maritime policymakers for assessing the scale of the problem.

Those authorities that failed to take corrective action were confronted with these reports each quarter. The reports were eagerly awaited by the shipping press, which exerted pressure on recalcitrant governments to act. No longer were governments able to hide behind the excuse of definitions and jurisdiction. This began to change the perception of the public and the media to the crime of piracy. Ship owners were also more willing to provide assistance to law enforcement agencies directly or through the IMB to assist in the prosecution of pirates.

The IMB Piracy Reporting Center became a catalyst for most antipiracy initiatives in the region. With Japan taking the lead on this issue, informal networks were built between law enforcement agencies dealing with this problem. All major maritime law enforcement agencies in Asia are now aware of the problem of piracy and are prepared to cooperate with each other in this area, often by an informal telephone call or fax message. This high degree of cooperation could perhaps not have been envisaged in 1991 when the Piracy Reporting Center was established.

The IMB Piracy Reporting Center has since become not just a source of information but a conduit through which prosecuting authorities seek information to build cases against offenders. Almost every major case of hijacking in the past two and a half years has resulted in the recovery of the vessel and, in recent cases, their crews and cargoes as well. In all these cases, the IMB Piracy Reporting Center played a key role, providing information, support, and liaison for the law enforcement agencies to act. By the law of percentages, the hijacking of ships is no longer a profitable exercise for the pirates.

A major advantage of a nongovernmental body running an initiative such as this is that it is not bound by the political sensitivities that bind a government. For example, an international business-sponsored information center can criticize a government for lack of effective law enforcement more easily than a neighboring country can. Law enforcement agencies should welcome constructive criticism from outside. It ensures that governments are pressured to allocate adequate resources and pass the necessary laws to help them deal with the problem. It may not always be possible for law enforcement agencies themselves to lobby successfully for these resources from within.

THE BUSINESS CYBER-CRIME MODEL

Although the mechanics of cyber crime—in terms of the frequency, ability to carry out an attack, and the fact an attack can originate from anywhere rather than a specific region—differ from the piracy situation, the basic tenets of the piracy model transfer well to the development of a framework for providing worthwhile information and bringing key issues to the fore.

What is different with respect to a prospective cyber-crime model is that the initial attitude of law enforcement in certain regions is not one of detachment or disinterest but, rather, uncertainty about how to tackle the problem. The less effective law enforcement is in combating cyber crime, the greater the number of attacks business is likely to suffer. With an ever-growing dependency on the Internet, it is no wonder that business is becoming increasingly concerned about the prospect of a corresponding explosion in crime involving information systems and the Internet. Victims not only face direct financial losses but may also incur increased insurance costs, negative publicity, loss of data, and exposure to criminal and civil liability.

The need for business to pool information on cyber crime is obvious. What sometimes prevents the free exchange of cyber-crime data is not the fear of negative publicity, however, but worries about providing competitors with commercially sensitive information.

An important role of a trusted third party is therefore to collect, analyze, and disseminate information, while at the same time keeping the source anonymous. There is no reason or need to identify the provider. A categorization of the sector in which the offense occurred and its modus operandi is more than sufficient for the analysis of trends and patterns and to alert business and law enforcement worldwide. A noncommercial business body is most likely to be seen by business as the most favored recipient of information as it has no competing interests. An organization that is viewed as a commercial competitor could stifle the free flow of data because of the perception, however unjust, that the information provided might give some commercial advantage to the recipient. One is reminded of the SEADOCS Registry designed and run by Chase Manhattan Bank in the early 1980s to act as a central reference point for bills of lading for oil cargoes. The motive and the concept were beyond reproach. Nevertheless one of the key reasons for its failure to get off the ground was that competing trade finance interests were not prepared to support a venture that gave Chase Manhattan such a key, high-profile role.

The International Chamber of Commerce (ICC), the world business organization, is ideally placed to provide this information. Trusted by business and respected by law enforcement, it could be the catalyst to push forward initiatives in this area.

A BUSINESS RESPONSE TO AN INTERNET FRAUD

During the past year we have witnessed a variety of attacks on businesses in the form of denial-of-service attacks, viruses/worms, intrusions, and the theft of proprietary information. Other forms of cyber crime include financial frauds and the sale of counterfeit goods and fake identification, the latter predominately U.S., on the Internet.

A good example of how a two-way exchange of information led to the discovery of a major cyber-crime fraud involved a multibillion-dollar fake financial instrument scam. This case is also interesting because, even though the fraudsters' efforts were frustrated, it did not result, as far as we are aware, in the perpetrators being identified and prosecuted.

The fraud, which relied on faking Web pages of Bloomberg and Euroclear (the international system for clearing securities and Eurobonds), was picked up after reports were made through the membership network of the Commercial Crime Bureau (CCB), which forms part of the ICC Commercial Crime Services.

The subsequent investigation revealed that an international group had constructed a complex fraud involving the sale of fake banking guarantees, appearing to be from 29 European banks, with face values of tens of millions of pounds.

The CCB was informed that advance fees of hundreds of thousands of dollars were paid for the issue of these fraudulent guarantees and that Web sites were used to validate the documents. The amounts represented on the fraudulent sites ranged from $50 million to more than $400 million. In addition to being used to procure advance fees, these guarantees were to be used in bogus high-yield investment programs (HYIP), which promised high returns from low-risk financial instrument trading.

As part of the sale of the bogus high-yield investment bonds, victims were shown Web sites sporting domain names such as www.euroclear30.50megs.com and www.bloomberg.50megs.com, where they would see a copy of the organizations' Web sites and information backing the fake financial instruments.

Through the ICC Commercial Crime Services member network, the bank guarantees were confirmed to be fraudulent, and Euroclear Bank and Bloomberg were alerted. On behalf of all parties concerned, the CCB coordinated the approach to the fraudster's Internet service provider, who complied with their request to shut down the offending sites. Shutting down fraudulent sites in cases such as this not only protects investors from scams; it also helps companies to maintain their reputation. The big risk is that this type of fraud could damage the trust on which the banking, finance, and insurance industries are built.

What would have completed the response to this fraud would have been the involvement of law enforcement authorities in pursuing those who had set up the fraudulent sites. It is hoped that the efforts of the sort of information center envisaged in the cyber-crime model, being a key element of the partnership between business, law enforcement, and government, would have been more effective in achieving this goal.

CONCLUSIONS

There is a vital need for relevant and timely statistical information on global cyber crime to be collated and disseminated to business, law enforcement agencies, and IT policymakers in governments. This will provide the building blocks on which strategies, policies, and international initiatives can be based. The dissemination of such relevant information on a regular basis will help to ensure that the eyes of the powers-that-be remain focused on the problem. Only with increased awareness and pertinent, timely data will solutions become achievable.

The most appropriate center for the receipt and dissemination of this vital information is one sponsored by business, to encourage the reporting of attacks. The center should then pass on the results of its analyses, free from political manipulation, bringing together the disparate strands of business, law enforcement, and government policymakers toward a common goal. Business interests should see the center as noncompetitive and acting on its behalf. This role fits an organ of the International Chamber of Commerce.

CHAPTER FOUR

FORMAL BILATERAL RELATIONSHIPS AS A MECHANISM FOR CYBER SECURITY

Robert S. Litt and Gordon N. Lederman

With a speed that would have been difficult to anticipate even a decade ago, the world has become dependent on information technology. Electronic networks now undergird the economies, governments, and societies of the developed nations and are spreading to the less developed world as well. Furthermore, information technology networks are decentralized, often lack authentication mechanisms, and generally were not designed with security in mind. For these reasons, the task of maintaining the security of information systems presents a policy challenge of unprecedented complexity. Cyber security cuts across traditional distinctions between the public and private sectors, and among many disparate functions of government such as law enforcement, intelligence, and the military. Moreover, the global nature of networks requires that governments engage each other across all these disparate functions in order that each may effectively safeguard its own cyber security.

This chapter explores some aspects of the use of formal bilateral relationships as a tool for international cooperation for cyber-security purposes. It begins by describing some of the unique problems of cyber security, then discusses some of the defining characteristics of formal bilateral relationships, and finally offers some observations on how formal bilateral relationships might most effectively be used to further cyber security.

THE NATURE OF THE PROBLEM OF CYBER SECURITY

The OECD Guidelines for the Security of Information Systems define cyber security as "the protection of the interests of those relying on information systems from harm resulting from failures of availability, confidentiality, and integrity."[1] Effective cyber security involves a number of separate activities:

- **Prevention.** States must protect information systems from penetration. This can involve modifying hardware or software, or fostering certain user behavior; it also requires the rapid communication of information about security flaws and intrusions.

- **Prohibition.** States must identify and prohibit conduct that threatens the security of information systems.

- **Prosecution.** States must be able to identify and apprehend violators, and collect adequate evidence to lead to their conviction.

This triad of activities is not unique to cyber security. For example, protecting banks from being robbed involves prevention activities (such as armed guards and Plexiglas teller screens), legal prohibitions, and law enforcement techniques (such as surveillance cameras, dye packs in money, and fingerprint evidence) that can lead to apprehension and conviction. Protecting information systems, however, presents an array of problems that protecting banks does not. Most importantly, cyber security is inherently a global endeavor because of the global nature of networks. It is as easy to launch an intrusion from outside a state as from within, so the cooperation of another state will likely be needed to apprehend and prosecute a cyber criminal. Indeed, because an intruder's trail of communication may go through several countries, tracing one may require an unprecedented degree of international cooperation.

International cooperation is complicated, however, because cyber security cuts across a wide range of government activities, including law enforcement, intelligence, national defense, diplomacy, commercial promotion, and technology. On the domestic level an effective national cyber-security plan therefore requires close cooperation between government agencies that have previously operated with relative independence: deconflicting law enforcement and intelligence operations; ensuring that law enforcement and the military cooperate in responding to cyber attacks of unknown origin and purpose; coordinating the efforts of law enforcement and other authorities to develop international cooperation mechanisms with a state's diplomatic strategy; and ensuring that the development of standards for products, services, and processes does not impede technological progress or economic growth.[2]

These complexities are reflected on the international level as well. For example, because some states may engage in cyber attacks as a matter of national intelligence or defense policy, they may be hesitant to offer unqualified cooperation to investigations of such attacks by target states. Efforts to standardize hardware or software to promote security may be perceived as covert attempts to gain national competitive advantage. And the relationship among law enforcement, military, and intelligence functions more generally, or the standards and procedures followed in law enforcement investigations more specifically, may vary greatly among affected states.

Cyber security also differs from traditional law enforcement or national security matters because of the importance of rapid action. The havoc that could result from an attack against critical information systems, and the transitory nature of digital evidence, require that detection of, and response to, cyber attacks occur almost instantaneously. Instantaneous action is difficult enough to achieve domestically, but the difficulties are magnified on the international level. The normal leisurely pace of international law enforcement cooperation[3] simply will not do in the context of cyber attacks. Intelligence and military reaction must also be instantaneous in order to detect and block cyber attacks from terrorists or hostile states.

FORMAL BILATERAL RELATIONSHIPS

A formal bilateral relationship is an agreement between two states set forth in a legal instrument that defines responsibilities and obligations in order to effectuate a particular purpose. It is a truism, but a useful one, to note that the defining characteristics of a formal bilateral relationship are that it is formal and bilateral. The degree of formality may vary from a treaty that (depending on domestic law) might require ratification by a signatory state's legislature to a memorandum of understanding between the executives of each state, but a formal agreement will be reflected in a document and will therefore have a lesser degree of flexibility than an informal relationship.

Today there are few if any formal bilateral relationships dealing specifically with cyber security. Yet such agreements have traditionally been a mainstay of international law enforcement cooperation, through the mechanisms of extradition and mutual legal assistance treaties (MLATs). Extradition treaties provide procedures by which states can obtain the return of persons charged with offenses; MLATs provide procedures by which states can obtain evidence that is located in other states.[4] Bilateral agreements are also common in the military context, either formal offensive or defensive alliances or "Status of Forces Agreements" that govern the presence of one state's armed forces in another state. Less commonly, formal bilateral agreements provide for the exchange of intelligence information. These existing agreements suggest some of the strengths and weaknesses of formal bilateral arrangements.

BILATERAL VERSUS MULTILATERAL RELATIONSHIPS

Bilateral relationships offer a number of advantages over multilateral relationships. First, a state can enter into a relationship with individual states of its choosing, rather than negotiating with a large number of states via a multilateral process. This degree of choice permits a state to calibrate precisely the obligations it is willing to accept according to the characteristics of the chosen partner; multilateral relationships, by contrast, usually require states to assume reciprocal obligations with a wide variety of other states. For example, because it is often difficult to tell at the outset whether or not a cyber attack is state-sponsored, a state may be willing to enter into a far more intimate relationship for investigating intrusions if the other party is a trusted ally with whom it already has an intelligence relationship. Similarly, states with compatible legal systems can accomplish law enforcement cooperation more easily than states whose legal systems contain very different procedural protections.

Bilateral agreements are also generally quicker to negotiate and may be easier to keep secret than multilateral ones if domestic procedures do not require that they be made public. They are thus better suited than multilateral relationships for relationships that a state does not want publicized. Moreover, the potential secrecy of bilateral relationships, combined with a state's ability to choose its partner, means that these relationships are particularly appropriate for sensitive matters such as intelligence sharing and military cooperation.

Bilateral negotiations are more likely than multilateral ones to produce detailed legal instruments setting forth rights and duties with adequate granularity. Because of the large number of states involved, multilateral negotiation processes may achieve no more than a lowest-common-denominator recitation of high-level principles, with little practical utility. Bilateral arrangements are also easier to change quickly to take account of technological developments and other rapid changes in the cyber environment.

On the other hand, bilateral relationships are best suited for matters that affect only the two signatory states rather than for problems that are truly global or even regional in nature. Where the solution to a problem requires cooperation from all or a great majority of states, bilateral agreements may be of limited utility, in the same way that individual states can undercut international sanctions against rogue states. The "free rider" effect exacerbates this problem, as states can sometimes obtain the benefits of a multilateral agreement without acceding to the treaty and incurring the burdens. Even where multilateral cooperation is preferable, however, bilateral agreements can be useful in their own right if achieving multilateral agreement is not realistic, if the two states involved are relatively important in dealing with the particular issue (for example, on nuclear nonproliferation issues, states that process nuclear technology), or if the bilateral agreement can serve as a model for a later multilateral one.

Bilateral agreements also can lead to a welter of inconsistent relationships. For example, differing procedures established through a series of bilateral agreements may impede a criminal investigation that is truly multinational in scope. And any effort to set international technological standards is far more difficult through a series of individual bilateral agreements than through a single multilateral one.

FORMAL VERSUS INFORMAL RELATIONSHIPS

A formal relationship defines the obligations of each signatory state with more precision and in a more binding fashion than an informal one. To alter its obligations pursuant to a formal agreement, a state must generally either follow the termination or modification clauses in the agreement or take the more extreme step of abrogating the agreement. Conversely, the formal nature of the relationship gives each state the comfort of knowing that the other party is also locked into the relationship via legal obligation. Thus, formal relationships create more predictable and routine expectations of compliance. Moreover, the fact that a state's obligations are clearly defined in an agreement may make it easier to secure the assistance of private third parties, which might otherwise be uneasy about the impact of cooperation with a foreign state. Finally, certain actions, particularly those that require modifications to the domestic law of a state, can be taken far more effectively pursuant to a formal agreement because the existence of a formal international obligation will support the state's efforts to modify its laws.

On the other hand, although formal bilateral relationships are easier to keep from the public eye than formal multilateral ones, informal relationships are easier still to conceal due to the absence of a legal instrument. In addition, if two states need to establish a relationship quickly, informal arrangements are generally easier to create than formal ones that require drafting and careful wordsmithing. Finally, creation of a formal relationship requires a degree of confidence in the other state's ability to fulfill its obligations. For example, if one state doubts another's ability to keep formal requests for judicial assistance secret when requested, or to act on them rapidly, it is not likely to make use of an MLAT; if a state doubts the good faith of another's request for information, it will likewise move away from formal cooperation. Informal relationships, which do not require binding reciprocity, can ease this friction.

SUITABILITY OF FORMAL BILATERAL RELATIONSHIPS TO THE CHALLENGE OF CYBER SECURITY

These general principles lead to the perhaps obvious conclusion that the usefulness of formal bilateral relationships likely depends in large part on the particular objective sought and the nations involved. Formal bilateral relationships are limited in their ability to tackle the full scope of the global challenge of cyber security, but may be effective for certain elements or in the short term given the relative speed with which such relationships can be established and the difficulty in achieving multilateral consensus. Policymakers will need to wrestle with the familiar question of whether, when comparing the merits of a complete multilateral solution with those of a more limited bilateral relationship, the best might be the enemy of the good.

PREVENTION

Effective cyber security requires not only the investigation and prosecution of cyber attacks after they occur, but the prevention of cyber attacks before they happen. Prevention is a complex goal, however. It requires substantial cooperation from the private sector, which must be encouraged or compelled to report vulnerabilities as they are discovered and intrusions as they occur. States may consider the establishment of standards for hardware and software, to ensure that they are secure, just as, for example, domestic law sets standards for automobile safety. They may also wish to encourage or compel certain behaviors such as password security, use of firewalls, and "patching" of vulnerabilities as they become known; insecure behavior in cyber space can harm not only the actor but also many other users "downstream" from a cyber attack.

These problems all exist on a domestic level, and states to date have not been particularly successful in solving them domestically. Speaking only of the United States, with which the authors are most familiar, private businesses remain extremely reluctant to share with government or with other businesses reports of vulnerabilities or attacks, for fear of competitive disadvantage, adverse public relations, or liability. Efforts by the government to set standards, most notably with respect to encryption, have failed abjectly, and no serious effort has been made to regulate individual behavior except by governments of their own users. Efforts to achieve international cooperation in this area thus may be premature.

On the other hand, international cooperation in this area remains essential. A state may be able to heighten its level of cyber security by purely domestic measures, but it can never assure complete cyber security without international cooperation, so long as unregulated persons outside its borders remain connected to the same networks. Ideally, of course, an international consensus would be reached, but such a consensus seems far from achievable at present. For a variety of reasons, therefore, formal bilateral agreements might be useful in advancing the goal of preventing cyber attacks. In particular, because a state can choose its partner in a bilateral relationship, it may be more comfortable with broader, deeper, and ultimately more-effective bilateral relationships with selected states in a number of respects:

- Because effective cyber security probably requires some sharing of information between states' intelligence services and between states' militaries, and also between those agencies and law enforcement, a state would likely agree to such information sharing only with its closest, trusted allies. Informality (and hence little or no public scrutiny) may be an advantage in dealing with the exchange of such sensitive information, however.

- Sharing of information concerning vulnerabilities, solutions, and best practices will also be facilitated if the states involved trust each other. Moreover, private- sector cooperation will be facilitated if states define, through a formal agreement, the uses to which such shared information will be put. And although information sharing among all states would be most valuable, bilateral information sharing can nevertheless be important. For example, some cyber attacks are calculated to occur automatically at a certain date and time; if states agree that those that are hit first will promptly share information with others, they could serve as a sort of "early warning" of cyber attacks—small consolation to the first victims but better for the world as a whole.

- States that seek to set hardware or software standards by international agreement will be more comfortable doing so if they are familiar with the technological level of their partner states. Even without an agreement that explicitly sets standards for the private sector, states whose governments have substantial purchasing power in the field of information technology may be able to influence the market as a whole by agreeing that they will procure only technologies that meet a particular standard or that their contractors must meet certain security standards. This could be done formally or informally, but domestic political difficulties (e.g., from disadvantaged competitors) would likely be more easily overcome with a formal agreement.

- States will be more likely to share research and development information with other states if they can be certain that the information will receive adequate intellectual property protection and that the recipient state will be able both to make use of the information and to provide useful information in return. Moreover, bilateral relationships are better suited to deal with the challenges posed by the dramatic rate of change in information technology; as new problems or solutions arise, a state would need to negotiate with only one other state to change the relationship rather than convene an international conference.

In short, although multilateral agreements might seem preferable in the abstract for dealing with the issue of prevention of cyber attacks, practical realities may, in the short run, favor bilateral action.

PROHIBITION

A key element of international cooperation in cyber security is ensuring that states enact prohibitions on cyber crime. The international nature of cyber crime makes it imperative that there be no "safe havens" from which hackers can conduct their attacks with impunity. The need for international unanimity in this area suggests that multilateral rather than bilateral agreements are preferable, and indeed the Council of Europe Convention on Cybercrime advances this goal.[5] Bilateral agreements among key states—those with the largest penetration of computer users—might be useful as well, but, as the experience with the Love Bug virus (which originated in the Philippines) showed, one cannot predict in advance where a cyber attack will originate. Bilateral agreements might also serve as a means of securing adherence to multilateral standards, by imposing sanctions on nations that do not effectively ban cyber attacks. A model here might be the activity of the Financial Action Task Force (FATF),[6] which has been successful in producing changes in the laws of alleged money-laundering havens; although the FATF is multilateral, bilateral agreements among key players with sufficient influence might accomplish similar results.

Formal agreements, as opposed to informal ones, have a significant advantage in this area. Our experience in the United States, at least, suggests that it is easier to pass enabling legislation if it is required by an international agreement and, conversely, that the formality of negotiations for international agreements allows for public input at an early stage, ensuring that whatever agreement is reached is politically palatable.

PROSECUTION

International cooperation in the detection, investigation, and prosecution of cyber crime is advancing rapidly, both bilaterally and multilaterally, but much remains to be done. On the most basic level, existing extradition treaties and MLATs must be examined to ensure that cyber crimes are covered offenses. Yet, as discussed above, the nature of cyber crime requires international cooperation of a nature and on a scale far beyond that involved in traditional crimes. "Real-time" exchange of law enforcement and, if appropriate, intelligence information is required, as is "real-time" execution of warrants to seize evidence, and to intercept communications or trace their origins. This requires not only formal steps to ensure that domestic legal procedures support these techniques, but less-formal ones to ensure that trained personnel are available at all times, that each state knows who to contact in the other state, and that the states' legal systems are capable of responding quickly. Consideration must be given to entirely novel approaches, such as the international recognition of warrants or the authorization of remote searches.

For a variety of reasons, multilateral agreement may be more difficult to achieve than bilateral agreement in the area of enforcement. National legal systems differ widely both in the procedures that they follow and in the extent to which they provide protections to targets. Domestic organic law may prohibit some states from providing certain kinds of cooperation to states that do not meet certain standards. Here again, a state's ability to pick its bilateral partners may enable more effective cooperation than could be accomplished through multilateral negotiations. For example, a state might be quite hesitant to enter into an agreement to execute search or arrest warrants from another state, unless it is entirely comfortable with the legal protections in its partner state. This applies both to a state's willingness to make requests for assistance, which requires a certain comfort that the request will be executed in a reliable and secure manner, and its willingness to obligate itself to respond to such requests, which requires a certain comfort in the good faith of, and legal basis for, the request and in the uses to which the response will be put.

Similarly, because of the potential overlap among law enforcement, intelligence, and national security in the investigation of cyber attacks, states may want to deal (at least initially) only with their most trusted allies in investigating such incidents. At the outset of an investigation, whether an intrusion is the work of a teenage or criminal hacker, an intelligence probe, or information warfare may be unclear, particularly because the immediate source of the attack may be a computer far removed from the attack's actual origin. States may wish to share more or less information depending on the state from which the attack appears to come, and bilateral rather than multilateral relationships better promote this sort of flexibility. Moreover, because formal relationships are generally reciprocal, a state is more likely to be willing to obligate itself to cooperate with a state with which it is friendly—and against whom it is hence less likely to be engaged in surreptitious activities of its own. Although international agreements may contain exceptions that permit a state to decline to cooperate based on its "national interest," a state would presumably prefer not to invoke such an exception, in effect admitting its own activities.

On the other hand, the defects of relying on bilateral cooperation are real. The global nature of information technology, and the ease of routing intrusions through servers anywhere on the globe, means that cyber criminals and cyber terrorists will flock to those states offering the most propitious havens, and they will avoid those known to cooperate vigorously in investigations. Relationships with states that already have adequate cyber-security legislation and procedures will be of little use when the attack comes from a state that lacks such legislation and procedures. Moreover, investigating a cyber attack that involves a number of different jurisdictions may be exceedingly complex if a variety of different bilateral agreements with a variety of different procedures must be invoked; a single multilateral framework would be far more efficient.

Both formal and informal bilateral relationships are important for the investigation and prosecution of cyber attacks. Formal mechanisms are probably necessary to ensure that evidence is gathered in a manner that is usable in the courts of the requesting state and to invoke legal processes to arrest and extradite a perpetrator. Moreover, formal relationships permit the advance establishment of procedures that can be invoked routinely in the event of an incident, rather than developing ad hoc solutions.

On the other hand, perhaps the most important aspect of international cooperation in enforcement is the building of individual relationships between key players in the various states. This can be done—and is being done today—most effectively on an informal level. Law enforcement and intelligence authorities can agree to staff cyber-security centers full time and to respond quickly to requests.

They can exchange information and ideas informally. And they can grow to have a trust and confidence in each other that will, in the long run, facilitate effective enforcement as much as any formal relationships.

Models for this sort of informal law enforcement cooperation exist in bilateral working groups (BWGs) that the United States has with a number of its close allies and neighbors. These BWGs convene representatives of a variety of law enforcement agencies from the two states to discuss problems of mutual interest. They can serve as a sounding board to propose and discuss solutions; they also help to build the personal relationships that make international cooperation effective. Another approach is the exchange of law enforcement personnel, through formal or informal agreements. The knowledge and relationships built during such exchanges facilitate effective cooperation.

CONCLUSION

The problem of cyber security is a daunting one, and one that changes almost on a daily basis. International cooperation is essential to cyber security, yet difficult to achieve. Above all, states must avoid locking themselves into unproductive approaches or approaches that lack the flexibility to adapt to the changing environment. Formal bilateral relationships can be a useful approach to this problem.

Notes

1. OECD Guidelines for the Security of Information Systems, § 4, set forth at http:// www.oecd.org/oecd/pages/home/displaygeneral/0,3380,EN-document-43-nodirectorate-no-6- 10249-29,FF.html.

2. See Presidential Decision Directive 63, May 22, 1998, set forth at http:// www.fas.org/irp/offdocs/pdd/pdd-63.htm.

3. Mutual legal assistance treaties (MLATs) and extradition treaties generally do not set forth specific time limits for a requested state's response, and certain states have arduous procedures for responding to another state's request, which delay the response. CarrieLyn Donigan Guymon, "International Legal Mechanisms For Combating Transnational Organized Crime: The Need For A Multilateral Convention," 18 *Berkeley Journal of International Law* 53, 83 (2000). See, for example, U.S.-Turkey Treaty on Extradition and Mutual Assis-

tance in Criminal Matters, entered into force January 1, 1981, 32 UST 3111, TIAS 9891. A list of MLATs into which the United States has entered may be found at http://travel.state.gov/mlat.html.

4. Informal means are sometimes used to accomplish the same ends. For example, the United States occasionally uses what it calls "rendition" to obtain custody of persons in foreign states, simply by transporting them to the United States with or without the cooperation of local authorities. In addition, informal cooperation between law enforcement agencies often fills the gap when no formal MLAT exists. The United States in particular has also aggressively and unilaterally expanded its domestic enforcement jurisdiction to compel the production of evidence held in foreign states by entities with a U.S. presence.

5. The convention was opened for signature on November 23, 2001. The text of the convention is set forth at http://conventions.coe.int/Treaty/en/Treaties/Word/185.doc.

6. Information about the FATF is set forth at http://www.oecd.org/fatf.

CHAPTER FIVE

EFFECTIVE TRANSNATIONAL MODELS OF COLLABORATION
BILATERAL FORMAL COOPERATION
Charles Lim Aeng Cheng

WHAT IS BILATERAL FORMAL COOPERATION?

Bilateral formal cooperation is a framework for cooperation that is usually between two parties or two countries and is formalized in legal documents such as a mutual legal assistance treaty (MLAT) or a memorandum of understanding (MOU). This bilateral cooperation is usually also characterized by supporting domestic legislation such as a mutual legal assistance act.

DIFFERENT LEVELS OF COOPERATION

There are various levels of cooperation. Firstly and obviously is cooperation between governments, and secondly is cooperation between agencies. The agency-to-agency level may work well in practice as it is likely that the police agency in one country would prefer to cooperate with the police agencies of the other countries, intelligence agencies with their intelligence counterparts, and so on. I would characterize this form of bilateral cooperation as being both formal and informal. In the private sector, we have the nongovernmental organization-to-nongovernmental organization (NGO) level of cooperation. For example, the ICRA

This chapter records the author's personal perspectives. His observations on this topic are of general application and are not intended to reflect the official views of the government of Singapore or the Attorney General's Chambers of Singapore.

(Internet Content Rating Association) is an example of cooperation at the nongovernmental level. And, in fact, many multinational corporations actually have their own information technology (IT) security departments that cooperate with each other. I've actually met a former Canadian police commissioner who after retirement was engaged as the head of the professional IT security department of a multinational corporation. This is an illustration of cooperation at the industry-to-industry level.

Formal vs. Informal Cooperation

Different types of assistance are available through formal versus informal cooperation. *Formal cooperation* often complements government-to-government cooperation. In contrast, *informal cooperation* faces a number of restrictions and limitations. For example, certain types of assistance may be available only through formal cooperation such as the execution of search warrants and cases requiring judicial process to compel production of witnesses, documents, or other evidence. The attendance of witnesses in foreign court proceedings obviously requires formal cooperation. If evidence is required for prosecution, such evidence can be used only if it can be admissible in court and carries sufficient evidential weight. Therefore, formal procedures are required to obtain and authenticate key evidence for admissibility in court. A formal framework can also provide for admissibility of evidence obtained from abroad and authenticated by a foreign judicial or other process. For example, a computer file authenticated by a foreign judicial representative can be made admissible even though it may otherwise be inadmissible under the "hearsay evidence" rule.

Formal cooperation can facilitate "active defense"[1] in the sense of the apprehension and extradition of fugitive offenders that is only possible through formal cooperation. Formal procedures may also be required to identify and confiscate the evidence or proceeds of a crime. This brings to mind the confiscation of drug trafficking proceeds mandated by the various United Nations conventions on psychotropic substances concluded in Vienna.[2] They also facilitate the new legal powers exercisable in cyber space, for example, lawful access to encrypted material. This is consistent with the new OECD (Organization for Economic Cooperation and Development) guidelines for cryptography, which allow for lawful access. Also, the USA Patriot Act 2001[3] (enacted in the aftermath of the September 11, 2001, tragedy) allows for search warrants and interception of communications.

Bilateral vs. Multilateral Cooperation

We must be realistic and recognize that the digital divide among nations may actually slow the multilateral process, especially as many nations lack capabilities and expertise in cyber security. Even in the highly integrated and developed European Union, the Council of Europe Cybercrime Convention, Budapest (November 23, 2001) took four years of negotiations to conclude. A multilateral convention at the United Nations level may well take two to three times that amount of time. Obviously, a bilateral process is a faster route to concrete results. And the framework can be implemented beginning with minimal operational requirements, for example, the establishment of 24/7/365[4] points of contact and graduating to more sophisticated, higher-level areas of cooperation. In addition, the bilateral approach can avoid the dilution that results from having to compromise to achieve multilateral consensus. Most diplomats would agree that the lowest common denominator is usually the point of agreement in multilateral negotiations. And that compromise may actually hinder the efficacy and workability of the convention, resulting in the omission of many cyber security measures that is more the result of ignorance than any deliberate action. This is because the less-developed countries and the less IT-enabled countries may actually obstruct certain initiatives purely because their authorities do not understand the technological aspects. People usually will not agree to things that they do not understand.

A lack of harmonization and different levels of maturity of cyber laws may also impede the multilateral route. The I Love You virus was traced back to a hacker in the Philippines, but the Philippine

National Bureau of Investigation had to drop charges because they had no cyber-crime law at that time. Since then, the Philippines has actually enacted an Electronic Commerce Act[5] based on the Singapore Electronic Transactions Act (Cap. 88). Section 48 of the Philippines act criminalizes cyber crime, so it is no longer a problem there. This is an illustration, however, of the differing levels of maturity of legal systems dealing with cyber security.

Bilateral negotiations are also confidential and more flexible. For example, several countries may be hesitant to share sensitive information when they are not so comfortable with the recipient country. The flexibility afforded by bilateral negations will also address the very important point made by the permanent secretary of our Ministry of Defense, Peter Ho, about keeping up with rapidly changing information technologies. It is also important because of the phenomenon of convergence—both horizontal and vertical.[6] For example, how do you characterize a certain event? Can it be classified as broadcasting or telecommunications or the Internet or other traditional media? We may face difficulty in characterizing which particular offense the violation of cyber security falls in within a multilateral framework. But the bilateral framework offers the flexibility to fine-tune the classifications to cover the latest developments in cyber security.

In addition, states are free, of course, to choose their bilateral partners. Agreements can be concluded quickly between willing and ready parties with mutual national interests. It is not only a question of trust but also a question of maturity of the technology and legal systems. The bilateral framework allows for reciprocity so there is no one-way flow. For example, there are countries that are less sophisticated in IT development and other countries that are more dependent on IT and accordingly more vulnerable to cyber attacks. Another advantage of the bilateral approach is that it avoids an open-ended set of potential partners. Here sovereignty is involved. The interesting perspective is that the bilateral approach involves strengthening sovereignty. And a country may be hesitant to surrender its sovereignty. The multilateral convention, which has an open-ended set of parties, means that any other country in the world can jump onto the bandwagon. And by virtue of the multilateral cooperation requirements, one country has no choice but to afford equal treatment and equal cooperation to every other country to which the convention applies.

Bilateral Cooperation on the Industry-to-Industry Level

Bilateral cooperation on preventive security measures and standards between industries is equally important. As mentioned, collaboration between public and private sectors is important, so we ought not forget that bilateral formal cooperation is also possible between various sectors in industry and not focus only on the government-to-government level of cooperation. Some examples are industry cooperation on cross-certification agreements and international Public Key Infrastructure (PKI) standards.

DISADVANTAGES OF BILATERAL COOPERATION

What are some of the disadvantages of the bilateral approach? There are actually several. The borderless nature of the Internet creates third-party havens and gaps. We have heard the fascinating account of denial-of-service attacks distributed over multiple countries using zombie computers. These attacks may be mounted in third-party countries that are not within the bilateral framework. Certain counties can therefore become havens for mounting cyber attacks by terrorists.

Of course, it is much more difficult for every government to develop a comprehensive network of bilateral agreements that are equal and consistent with each other. Inconsistency between different bilateral agreements may emerge. A bilateral formal framework could, however, complement the multilateral framework. A network of bilateral arrangements against a backdrop of multilateral arrangements is also possible, for example, free trade agreements concluded bilaterally against the framework of the World Trade Organization (WTO) agreements.

TYPICAL REQUIREMENTS IN A BILATERAL
LEGAL FRAMEWORK

There are some typical requirements in bilateral legal frameworks such as dual criminality. To achieve harmonization of equivalent cyber laws, the act must be an offense in both states in the bilateral agreement. This would also help avoid frivolous requests. The legal framework should also have adequate protection of human rights and fundamental liberties of witnesses and accused persons; for instance, a particular individual may suffer costly expenses if he is required to produce evidence in a foreign country.

In fact, it is interesting to note (coming back to the harmonization of laws) that prior to 1998, a distributed denial-of-service attack would not have been an offense under Singapore's Computer Misuse Act. And neither would password trafficking—getting someone's password and posting it on the Internet for the whole world to see. An example would be if someone legitimately obtains a password to a Cray supercomputer and posts it on the Internet for the whole world to try to hack into the computer. Those two acts would not have been an offense under Singapore's laws prior to 1998 for the simple reason that no unauthorized access would have been gained by the culprit into any computer system. However, in 1998 we fixed that to make the distributed denial-of-service attacks against computers and the trafficking of passwords an offense. So imagine that if two different countries have different cyber-law offenses, there could be a problem of harmonization of cyber laws, especially when a cyber attack mounted across multiple borders could be treated as a cyber-crime offense in one country but not in another.

Standard of proof is another issue. To protect human rights and avoid frivolous requests, there should be a minimum standard of proof—a prima facie case to support the request—or at least an ongoing investigation by the requesting country. One approach is to include cyber-security offenses in a list of offenses covered by a framework. It is helpful for police and law enforcement authorities to know precisely what offenses they are investigating. On the other hand, such an approach may lack technology neutrality: The list may not be adequate in the light of more recent developments in technology.

To preserve the sovereignty and national integrity of individual countries, we need a framework that preserves the discretion to refuse full cooperation to the requesting countries if it is against the public interest. Similarly, there should be discretion to refuse the request if the offense is minor, or an offense of a political character, or where there is discrimination based on race, religion, gender, et cetera.

SINGAPORE'S LEGAL FRAMEWORK

Singapore has a Mutual Assistance in Criminal Matters Act (Cap. 190A). The predecessor act to this was the Singapore Drug Trafficking (Confiscation of Benefits) Act 1993,[7] and the attorney general is designated as the central authority in the act. We are considering bilateral agreements with some countries. One problem, however, is that these agreements may not yet extend to cyber crime. In the beginning stages, we are focusing on drug trafficking and other conventional serious crimes.

Last, I would like to mention the extraterritorial jurisdiction provision in Singapore's Computer Misuse Act (Cap. 50A). This provision (Section 11) would allow a person who hacks into a computer located in Singapore to be apprehended and punished as if he had committed the act in Singapore. Similarly, if a hacker in Singapore hacks into a computer in the United States, that Singapore hacker can be punished in our courts even though the physical act of hacking may have taken place in the target computer in the United States. This approach is used because it avoids messy extradition proceedings and there is no need for the requesting country to bear the cost of imprisonment or the punishment.[8]

An example: A 15-year-old boy from a neighboring country hacked into the server in Singapore belonging to the Data Storage Institute of the National University of Singapore (NUS) while he was a student in Australia. He was foolish enough later on to come to Singapore to study at one of our local schools, and he again hacked into the NUS computer. He was apprehended, and he was charged on July 20, 2000, in the Juvenile Court not only for the offenses of hacking in Singapore, but also for hacking into a Singapore computer from Australia. He pleaded guilty to all charges.[9] This was the first time we invoked this extra-territorial jurisdiction provision. In that case, we were able to apprehend and punish the suspect without the need for formal extradition proceedings. It would be useful if two countries had this type of jurisdiction because that would allow one county to inform the other of the existence of the fugitive and allow the other country to punish the fugitive without the need for extradition.

Notes

1. "Active defense" by definition imposes serious risk or penalty on the attacker and is a term used by Professor Seymour Goodman of the Georgia Institute of Technology in his paper "Toward a Treaty-Based International Regime on Cyber Crime and Terrorism." (See chapter 6.)

2. UN Convention on Psychotropic Substances, Vienna, 1971, and UN Convention against Illicit Traffic in Narcotic Drugs and Psychotropic Substances, Vienna, 1988.

3. Uniting and Strengthening America by Providing Appropriate Tools Required to Intercept and Obstruct Terrorism Act (October 24, 2001).

4. Slang term for 24 hours a day, 7 days a week, 365 days a year.

5. Republic Act No. 8792.

6. Horizontal convergence refers to convergence of technology platforms; vertical convergence refers to convergence of processes and content.

7. Extensively amended and renamed in 1999 as the Corruption, Drug Trafficking and Other Serious Crimes (Confiscation of Benefits) Act (Cap. 65A).

8. Under Section 11 of the Singapore Computer Misuse Act, in both cases there is a clear nexus with Singapore and the assertion of jurisdiction can be justified in accordance with the nationality or protective principles. It could even be argued that the offense had actually taken place in Singapore in either scenario, as the target of the cyber attack is located in Singapore in the first scenario, and in the second scenario the acts were carried out by the offender in Singapore.

9. Reported in the *Straits Times* (Singapore), July 21, 2000.

CHAPTER SIX

TOWARD A TREATY-BASED INTERNATIONAL REGIME ON CYBER CRIME AND TERRORISM
Seymour E. Goodman

CYBER DEFENSE IN A TRANSNATIONAL ENVIRONMENT

It is often said that cyberspace is borderless, and in some ways it has erased borders between countries. Conversely, global connectivity has made it possible for attackers to work from almost any country against targets in almost every country, and because all of cyberspace comes to ground somewhere, it has essentially created "borders" between every pair of countries, not just those that are physically adjacent.

Thus almost every country is, or potentially is, part of the problem of cyber security in a global age. Most national and local governments are incapable of dealing with, and often are largely unaware of, the difficulties of cyber disruption. Helping to make them part of the solution is desirable. Most are technically and otherwise incapable of doing this on their own. Because much of the problem of cyber crime and terrorism is intrinsically transnational, some form of international cooperation arguably should be part of the national strategies of most of the 200-plus governments of the world whose countries are connected to the Internet and other networked infrastructures.

This chapter will consider the need for, the characteristics of, and some of the difficulties that will have to be worked out in the pursuit of a treaty-based, multilateral regime as a form of international coordination and cooperation to help prevent and respond to cyber crime and terrorism.[1] We will be concerned with acts against cyber

systems (e.g., destroying, incapacitating, trespassing against, interfering with, or misusing them[2]).

For the purposes of a formal multilateral treaty, we take the view
that it is both difficult and unnecessary to precisely define "cyber terrorism." There is unlikely to be much agreement among a wide spectrum of interested parties on such a definition given the enormous
variety of malicious activity possible in this medium and the range of
motivations behind the spectrum of possible attacks. Distinguishing
an early stage of an attack as either crime or terrorism is difficult, and
even the final determination may depend on the "eyes of the be-
holder." We take the approach of defining serious forms of crimes
against information systems under the assumption that essentially all
forms of what would widely be considered cyber terrorism would be
egregious instances of these crimes. Furthermore, we add to the list
of serious offenses "the uses of a cyber system as a material factor in
committing an act made unlawful or prohibited" by a number of
widely adopted international conventions intended to deal with terrorism (e.g., the International Maritime Organization Convention
for the Suppression of Unlawful Acts against the Safety of Maritime
Navigation [Maritime Terrorism Convention] of March 10, 1988).[3]
As is the case in other contexts—for example, safety and security in
civil aviation—the nature of the attack itself is what matters; the mo-
tivation of the attacker should not be a determining factor.

We define and distinguish between two complementary forms of
defense:

- **Passive defense** is essentially target hardening. It consists
  largely of the internal use of various technologies and products
  (e.g., firewalls, cryptography, intrusion detection) and procedures (e.g., those governing outside dial-in or reconstitution
  and recovery) to protect the information technology (IT) assets
  owned by an individual or organization. Some forms of passive
  defense may be dynamic (e.g., stopping an attack in progress).
  By definition, however, passive defense does not impose serious
  risks or penalties on the attacker. With only passive defensive
  measures, the attacker is free to continue to assault the target

until he either succeeds or gets frustrated and looks elsewhere. Given the vulnerabilities of most cyber systems and the low cost of most attacks, a skilled and determined attacker may be more likely to succeed than become frustrated.

- **Active defense** by definition imposes serious risk or penalty to the attacker. Risk or penalty may include identification and exposure, stopping an attack in progress, investigation and prosecution, or preemptive or counterattacks of various sorts.

Note that some defensive actions, for example stopping an attack in progress, can be pursued using both passive and active means. Passively, the defender might plug a vulnerability hole in real time. Actively, the defender might try to get back at the source of the attack.

In the transnational context, passive defense is not without problems—with regard to liability, negligence, controls on cryptography, or information sharing, for example. The pursuit of active defensive measures in an international context is more difficult, however, and will get most of the attention in the remainder of this chapter.[4]

At the very least, active defense involves gathering information about the attacker. It can go well beyond that to damaging the attacker's cyber assets to physically apprehending or otherwise physically incapacitating the attacker. Because all of cyberspace "comes to ground" somewhere, including at sea, all attackers and their assets are essentially located within the jurisdictions of one or more nation-states. For a defender to engage in unilateral active defense in almost any transnational context, he will likely have to (perhaps covertly) reach into computers, telecommunications channels, and other places physically located outside his legal jurisdiction.

Because private sectors around the world own, operate, and use much of the information infrastructure, they and their assets are, and will continue to be, primary targets. Many private entities are technically capable of trying to engage in active defense. They do not have a legal basis for doing so in an international context, however, and the state of technology is such that the likelihood that they may incorrectly identify their attackers, cause undesirable collateral damage, or make some other kind of mistake is considerable. In so doing, they may become more serious and more readily identifiable offenders than their attackers, and may be subject to considerable liability, negative publicity, and criminal penalties. Furthermore, few governments anywhere officially condone vigilantism.

Thus the pursuit of active defense necessarily falls to governments. Governments are not subject to the liability risks of private entities. A good case can be made to the effect that national governments would be justified in engaging in active defense under the international legal principles of proportionality and response-in-kind.[5] Yet few, if any, nations would welcome another government's intrusions into information systems located within their sovereign domain without their permission, and the intruding government would largely have to do so covertly. Under these circumstances, particularly if the volume of serious cyber attacks is high, sooner or later visible misidentifications and collateral damage will result, and they would likely generate international friction between governments. The government engaging in active defense would also be at a serious disadvantage with regard to apprehending or otherwise physically dealing with the attackers. Furthermore, for any country to establish precedents for aggressive international behavior in this arena would seem unwise.[6]

The government of the United States, in particular, should have reservations in this regard. Because of presumed technical prowess and other reasons, it will be held to higher standards of accountability and suspicion than other governments. It will suffer serious blame in public opinion and elsewhere when its intrusions inevitably result in undesirable collateral or other damage. The United States is home to far more information systems and hosts much more of the Internet than any other country. It is physically home to a larger number of attackers and is a third-party transit country for more network traffic than any other country. As such, eventually it is likely to be a target of a great many active defensive measures by other countries, and we might expect some fraction of these to be carried out relatively incompetently. We can be sure that the U.S. government, not to mention the private-sector owners, operators, and users of these information systems, will very much resent such intrusions by other governments. We cannot imagine that the governments or private sectors of any of the other countries present at this conference would be too happy with the prospect of unilateral U.S.-based measures being implemented in their territories without consent.

FINDING A SUITABLE FRAMEWORK FOR INTERNATIONAL COOPERATION

These arguments and constraints lead us to conclude that the *ideal* international arrangement would look something like the following. First, each of the governments of the world would have substantial competence to deal with the problem of preventing and punishing attacks on cyber systems. This includes capabilities and policies in passive defense to provide effective security for those portions of cyberspace within each government's purview. Second, all connected countries would share a common baseline perception of what constitutes serious (felony) criminal behavior in this new medium. One of the manifestations of this shared perception would be a similar set of laws defining such behavior and offenses in each country.[7] Third, each would have substantial capability in active defense, and a competent national authority for engaging in active defense. Finally, a near-universal umbrella convention that would permit timely action among any combination of countries, under established procedures, would cover international responses to transnational attacks.

Under these ideal circumstances, we might expect the following standard scenario if a serious cyber attack is launched from Country X against targets in Country A. The victims in A immediately seek help from Government A. Government A determines that there is reason to suspect that the attack originated from, or at least passed through, X. Under the umbrella international convention, Government A immediately contacts the competent authority in X, where the attack is equally viewed as a crime. Government A can count on Government X's willingness and ability to investigate the extent to which the attack is taking place from X. The competent authority in X will act in a timely manner to help stop the attack and proceed with other forms of defense in essentially the same way that Government A would if it had the jurisdictional authority to do so itself (albeit subject to such differences in human and civil rights as may exist), or it would permit Government A or an international organization to participate directly or in an advisory capacity.

Because of all the ideal commonalities under the near-universal arrangement just described, this procedural scenario scales. So, for example, it extends in a straightforward manner if the attack is simultaneously launched from Countries X, Y, and Z against targets in Countries A and B, and the attack is routed through M, N, P, and Q.

As far as we can determine, this is the *only unambiguously legal* way to handle active defense on the global scale of the Internet and other large transnational networks. It is also the only way we can conceive of to avoid the possibility of an enormous amount of largely covert actions on the parts of governments against systems and citizens in other countries. It would tend to minimize the errors, collateral damage, and other forms of friction that might arise between nations as a result of that covert activity.

The present reality is far from this ideal situation. Perhaps most importantly, the great majority of the governments of the more than 200 countries or other semi-sovereign entities with Internet connectivity have little awareness, and less capability, in this area.

So how may we proceed from the current reality to something closer to the ideal international situation? We would argue that we should start to think about the desired structure and content of such an international convention. The time scales associated with conducting and dealing with malicious cyber activities varies from weeks (e.g., the time for new tactical attack modes to emerge) to the comparatively glacial time scales for building extensive and effective international agreements. So it is necessary to start thinking about the long and iterative process of the latter, even though it is too early to expect solutions to some specific and difficult problems and questions. We might look to a framework that builds in an expectation and means for dealing with the detailed problems of changing technology during an essentially unbounded time into the future, as well as one intended to help build the capabilities of weaker countries.

What might be included as necessary top-level features in such an international regime? We would suggest the following:[8]

- The focus should be on *serious crimes against computer networks.* The primary concern is protecting the infrastructure, both the IT-based infrastructure itself and the other infrastructures that may be accessed and damaged or manipulated through IT-based control structures. This, we believe, is not the place to address content crimes and issues (e.g., pornography or intellectual property rights).

- There should be a *harmonization of laws.* Each state party to the convention must adopt a complete set of national laws defining and punishing the full range of serious crimes against computer networks. Although the wording of these laws need not be identical for each country, each must establish all of the collectively defined malicious behavior specified in the agreement as felonies within the country. Having such a set of laws enacted would be a necessary condition for admission to the convention. We believe that this would also be sufficient for most extradition purposes. It is necessary to get near congruence of national laws widely accepted and to make the subject a formal, legitimate concern on an extensive international scale.

- There should be a *near-universal set of states parties.* The problem is intrinsically global, and at least some element of a partial solution must be global. Near-universal participation makes the problem legitimate globally and tries to eliminate safe havens. Each country connected to the Internet is part of the threat and vulnerabilities problems, and an effort must be made to try to make each a part of the solution. This is decidedly not the case now.

- A major goal should be to *build international capabilities* to deal with the problem. To this end we would propose a working organization, perhaps somewhat similar to the International Civil Aviation Organization for the transportation infrastructure, to help develop standards and best practices and to provide training and technology on a global scale, and especially for the large number of countries that have little or no capacity to do everything for themselves in the cyber domain at this time. This applies to both passive and active means of defense. Another partial model for a useful organization in this context may be the Internet Engineering Task Force, a volunteer and very public organization that is essentially the keeper and modifier of the basic Internet protocols. We tentatively call this organization the Agency for Information Infrastructure Protection (AIIP).[9]

- *Avoid building too much technical or procedural detail into the basic agreement.* At this time, nobody understands the technological and procedural means or costs well enough to appreciate what it would take to require them on a large scale. It will take some time for thoughts and technology to mature to the point where such might be recommended or required. We recommend setting up a forum and means (e.g., through the AIIP) for the necessary discussions and work to take place. As is the case in other international domains, industry and academic participation in these efforts would be essential.

- The prospective convention is *not meant to apply to the actions of states.* We suspect that there are dozens of nation-states investigating the possibilities of so-called information warfare or information operations. Few of those would presumably be interested in constraining themselves at this early stage. This is not meant to be an arms control convention, just as the various widely accepted agreements on safety and security in civil aviation (among other areas) are not meant to apply to the air forces of the nation states of the world with regard to their national security activities.

- States parties would *not violate the civil or human rights* of its citizens. No state party would be expected to compromise its own laws in this regard. So, for example, assume that both the United States and Iran are signatories. Say that a U.S. citizen is suspected of attacking an Iranian system in a manner that is against the laws that both countries have agreed on as part of signing the convention. If the United States suspects that this person's human rights would be at risk if extradited to Iran, then the United States is obligated to try that person for that crime in the United States, or to extradite him for trial to a third country that has a claim to jurisdiction but observes civil or human rights laws similar to those in the United States. In this regard, we observe that a harmonization of laws in the form of defining felonies does not also necessarily imply a harmonization of investigative law or procedures. Although some progress may be made to harmonize laws and procedures that pertain to privacy, seizure of assets, permitted incarceration periods without charge, etc., significant differences among countries will remain.

We briefly note that our views on several of these points differ to greater or lesser extent from those expressed or omitted in the convention adopted by about 30 members (and a few nonmembers) of the Council of Europe (COE).[10] We feel that the COE convention is focused too much on matters of prosecution and content violation, and we also believe it does not address several of the features above.[11]

We also note that reasonably effective agreements exist in other domains along the lines enumerated above. Perhaps the closest analogy is with civil aviation, which also happens to be extensively and increasingly dependent on cyber systems.[12] Other such agreements cover intrinsically transnational domains, such as maritime transportation, health, and pollution. We are a long way from having such an agreement for actions in cyberspace, and there will be considerable difficulties along any path to an effective approximation. We touch on a few of the problems below.

- As with many international agreements, questions arise as to forms of enforcement and sanctions against signatories who are not meeting the conditions or who are in conscious violation.

- The costs of such a convention must be estimated. Just two examples of such costs include an estimate of the volume and prospective growth rates of requests and investigations that would need to be handled, and the cost of establishing and running an organization like the AIIP and the competent national authorities. In terms of savings, we note that major cyber attacks (e.g., via virus or denial of service) have been estimated to cost hundreds of millions of dollars. So, as in the case with averted airline disasters, every prevented major incident represents a huge savings.

- As noted earlier, much of active defense is intelligence intensive. How will information and evidence be effectively shared among a diverse set of affected parties without compromising national interests?

- Private organizations—commercial Internet service providers (ISPs), for example—are key players in the global information infrastructures. Their cooperation and technology would be crucial to the effectiveness of any international regime to protect and assure those infrastructures. Many are extensively multinational in their operations. Who would they have to respond to? Where do their responsibilities and liabilities lie if there are many competing governments with different laws (e.g., on privacy, requests data, and other forms of cooperation)?

- How do we effectively scale up to a near universal sign-up? In addition to the obvious approach of simply starting with a small number of countries, possibilities include the use of more limited agreements as building blocks to acquire subsets of partners and experience with what works. These more limited agreements might be done bilaterally or multilaterally, based on sector (e.g., for the cyber dimensions of civil aviation) or regional (e.g., for Europe) domains.[13]

- In this regard, we might observe that a set of bilateral agreements will be unworkable as a long-term solution. Global connectivity enables too many countries. For N countries, a complete set of bilaterals that would allow any two to work together would require $\frac{N(N-1)}{2}$ agreements. In our case, N is approximately 220, necessitating 24,090 bilateral agreements. If one recognizes that attacks could involve three or more countries, the number of trilateral and multilateral agreements short of a universal agreement approaches 2^N.

- A related question is what to require of a state party as a condition for admission. Two possibilities are a set of harmonized domestic laws and the existence of a designated competent authority. Another related issue is what to do with the nonsignatories. For example, should (could) an effort be made to create a form of quarantine?

The "normal" model for international cooperation as described above has the AIIP as a derivative of the convention (i.e., as a body "enabled" by the convention much as the ICAO is enabled by the international conventions for civil aviation). Broad-based multilateral conventions are very hard to establish, however, and often take a long time. One way of dealing with several of the problems noted above may be to "put the cart before the horse" by establishing an AIIP along the lines of the Internet Engineering Task Force (IETF) or the Computer Emergency Response Teams (CERT) models before the international convention is established.[14] The AIIP could establish itself as a useful and respected organization, provide a vehicle for working with the private sector in this subject area, and form a nucleus around which the signatory nations could "condense" as the international convention develops. Initial funding would not have to come from some sort of tortuous process of securing funding from multiple governments to set up another diplomatically crafted Geneva-based agency. It could be established by industry or by limited and essentially detached U.S. government funds (as was the case with what was essentially the early IETF predecessor or the CERT) or by detached funding from a small number of governments or foundations, with the intent of having it taken under the international convention in time.

In 2002, President George W. Bush approved the Protocol to the Convention on Long-Range Transboundary Air Pollution dealing with Persistent Organic Pollutants (POPs). In so doing, the president cited three conclusions.

- First, he said that solid, scientific information has established the need to regulate POPs.

- Second, the problem is global in dimension, and it therefore requires a global response. The pollutants, the president said, "respect no boundaries and can harm Americans even when released abroad."

- Third, Bush appreciated that the protocol took into account the concerns of less-developed states; some needed time and help to achieve the agreed standards. The president praised the high level of cooperation among governments, businesses, and environmental groups that led to the treaty. The protocol relied heavily on business and scientific expertise to develop the best practicable methods and standards.

The president's appraisal is sound. It provides criteria by which to judge whether a transnational response is required to deal with a problem, and if so, how to structure a response to achieve its objectives.[15]

Judged by these criteria, we believe that protecting the citizens of all of the countries of the world from cyber crime and terrorism clearly requires an international regime, and that some kind of extensive convention is probably inevitable if both cyber space and malicious activity in this medium continue to rapidly expand globally. Given the time scales involved and how long it takes to work out effective agreements, not to mention some difficult issues that need to be resolved, we believe it is prudent to pursue serious deliberations on the matter.

Notes

1. An early version of this chapter was presented at the Russian Academy of Sciences–National Academy of Sciences (USA) Workshop on Terrorism in High-Tech Society and Modern Methods for Prevention and Response, Moscow, June 4–6, 2001, and will appear in a volume to be published by the National Academy Press. The present version is a significant revision and extension. The author is grateful to Dr. David Elliott, Dr. William Hoehn, Dr. Stephen Lukasik, and Judge Abraham Sofaer for their reviews and constructive comments.

2. These offenses are defined more explicitly in Articles 3 and 4 in Abraham D. Sofaer et al., *A Proposal for an International Convention on Cyber Crime and Terrorism* (Stanford, Calif.: Center for International Security and Cooperation, Stanford University), August 2000. Article 1, Paragraph 2, which unnecessarily attempts to define "cyber terrorism," should be considered deleted.

Hereafter this draft convention will be referred to as the Stanford Draft. More general and extensive coverage of the international aspects of cyber crime and law may be found in Abraham D. Sofaer and Seymour E. Goodman, eds., *The Transnational Dimensions of Cyber Crime and Terrorism* (Stanford, Calif.: Hoover Institution Press, 2001).

3. An explicit and extensive list of these conventions is provided in Article 3, Paragraph 1(f) of the Stanford Draft (cf. footnote 3).

4. For further discussion of active defenses from a legal perspective, see Gregory D. Grove, Seymour E. Goodman, and Stephen J. Lukasik, "Cyber-attacks and International Law," *Survival* 42, no. 3 (Autumn 2000): 89–103.

5. Jack Goldsmith, "Cybercrime and Jurisdiction," presented at the Conference on International Cooperation to Combat Cyber Crime and Terrorism, Stanford University, December 6–7, 1999.

6. Such issues are already becoming problematic. See, for example, Mike Brunker, "Cyberspace Evidence Seizure Upheld: FBI Downloaded Data from Suspects' Computers in Russia," MSNBC, May 30, 2001.

7. A project under the purview of the American Bar Association is attempting to put together a model set of appropriate cyber laws in this regard: International Cybercrime Project, American Bar Association, Science and Technology Section, Computer Law Division, Privacy and Computer Crime Committee, http://www.abanet.org/scitech/computercrime/home.html. An explicit set of offenses is also given in the Stanford Draft, Articles 3 and 4 (footnote 3 above).

8. Sofaer et al., *A Proposal for an International Convention on Cyber Crime and Terrorism*, discussed throughout the text.

9. The AIIP is first defined in the Stanford Draft. For some further discussion on its functions, makeup, etc., see S. J. Lukasik, "What Does an 'AIIP' Do?" presentation notes, Georgia Institute of Technology, Atlanta, Ga., May 27, 2000.

10. European Committee on Crime Problems, Committee of Experts on Crime in Cyber Space, Council of Europe. Draft Convention on Cyber Crime, http://conventions.coe.int/treaty/EN/cadreprojects.htm.

11. For a critique of Draft 25 of the COE convention, see Abraham D. Sofaer, "Responding to Transnational Cyber Crime," presented at the Workshop on Protecting Cyberspace, sponsored by the Georgia Tech Information Security Center (Georgia Institute of Technology) and the Center for International Security and Cooperation (Stanford University), Washington, D.C., May 1, 2001. A copy of this paper may be obtained from the present author.

12. See S. Goodman, M. Cuellar, and H. Whiteman, chapter 3 on civil aviation, in Sofaer et al., *The Transnational Dimensions of Cyber Crime and Terrorism*.

On the surface the case of civil aviation would seem to be simpler, at least partly because its defense is more discrete in that there is a much smaller number of targets (aircraft and airports), and these are physically easy to locate. It should also be noted that civil aviation is heavily dependent on information systems for many functions.

13. Hal Whiteman, "International Institutions and Agreements to Combat Serious Cyber Crime," presentation at the Workshop on Protecting Cyberspace, Washington, D.C., May 1, 2001.

14. Stephen J. Lukasik, private communication, June 28, 2001, suggested this inverted approach.

15. Sofaer, "Responding to Transnational Cyber Crime," 1–2.

CHAPTER SEVEN

EUROPE AND CYBER SECURITY
Stefano Rodotà

THE LEGAL FRAMEWORK

The system for personal data protection currently in force in Europe is the outcome of a stepwise process that has been going on for many years. There are a few fundamental strongholds in this system; it is, however, still under construction because it requires adjustments to an ever-changing reality. The final target has never been simply the establishment of common rules for different countries, as is typical with any international treaty. Indeed, the European Union being also a political entity, the final target cannot but also consist in creating a "law area" that is homogeneous in itself and regulates the manner of transferring personal data across its borders. This is why conventional international treaties with free accession clauses are accompanied by instruments drafted by the European Union that are binding on member states.

An initial set of common rules was devised by the Council of Europe, an international organization that includes a higher number of member states than the 15-member-strong European Union. The council's conventions are usually also open for the signature of nonmember states. The starting point was the 1950 European Convention on Human Rights, under Article 8 of which everyone has the right to respect for his private and family life. This principle was developed further by Convention No. 108 of 1981, which specifically concerns the protection of individuals with regard to automated processing of personal data, as well as by many recommendations applying, for instance, to data collected for scientific research and statistical purposes, health-related data, data collected for social security purposes, direct marketing data, data concerning payments, those processed by public bodies, data collected by means of genetic tests or screening, and telecommunications data. Enhanced protection of genetic data was provided for by the 1997 Convention on Human Rights and Biomedicine. Finally, the Cybercrime Convention of November 23, 2001, should be also referred to.

The rights enshrined in Council of Europe conventions may be claimed before the European Court of Human Rights in Strasbourg by the citizens of those states that have ratified the conventions. (Recommendations have no binding force.) These rights may be limited by such measures as may be necessary in a democratic society for the protection of national and public security, for the economic welfare of the country, for the prevention of disorder or crime, or for the protection of health, morals, rights, and freedoms of third parties. No reference to economic welfare and morals is made in the biomedicine convention.

As regards the legislative framework set up in the European Union, the basic reference is to Directive No. 46 of 1995 on the protection of individuals with regard to processing personal data and the free movement of such data. This directive set the foundations for a veritable common legal system in all member states by laying down the conditions for streamlined protection, not only in respect to EU citizens but also to any person whose data are processed in the EU. The principles set forth in this directive were specified further by Directive No. 66 of 1997 concerning the telecommunications sector, which is currently under revision. Additionally, they are expressly referred to in the e-commerce directive, wherein it is actually stated that the criteria set forth in Directive 94/46 are to be complied with.

Starting from the provisions made in these directives, which are binding on member states, national laws also have been enacted so as to ensure the protection of personal data by way of the activity of courts and independent authorities. The highest possible level of protection is to be guaranteed. Under Article 1 of Directive 95/46, the protection of personal data is regarded as an instance of the more general protection of fundamental rights and freedoms: "In accordance with this Directive, Member States shall protect the fundamental rights and freedoms of natural persons, and in particular their right to privacy with respect to the processing of personal data."

The end point of this enhanced protection is currently represented by the Charter of Fundamental Rights of the European Union, which was proclaimed in Nice in December 2000 and refers to privacy in two basic articles, namely:

Article 7. Respect for Private and Family Life—Everyone has the right to respect for his or her private and family life, home, and communications.

Article 8. Protection of Personal Data—

- Everyone has the right to the protection of personal data concerning him or her.

- Such data must be processed fairly and for specified purposes and on the basis of the consent of the person concerned or some other legitimate basis laid down by law. Everyone has the right of access to data that has been collected concerning him or her, and the right to have it rectified.

- Compliance with these rules shall be subject to control by an independent authority.

DATA PROTECTION AND "CONSTITUTIONALIZATION" OF INDIVIDUALS

In light of the provisions described above, the European Union can currently be regarded as the region in the world where the protection of personal data has reached the highest degree of particularization, in both qualitative and quantitative terms. As has already been pointed out, this exercise reached its final stage when the Charter of Fundamental Rights was adopted. Indeed, even though the charter is not legally binding, it can undoubtedly contribute to defining the set of fundamental rights referred to in Article 6.2 of the European Union Treaty.

The protection of personal data has therefore been recognized to be a fundamental human right (see Article 8 in the charter), to be kept separate from the conventional right to the protection of private and family life (the subject of Article 7). Significantly, the charter does not simply proclaim the right to the protection of personal data, but specifies its contents and refers to a tool for enforcing that right—that is to say, control by an independent authority.

The resulting legal framework can therefore be said to envisage support for and integration of the individual's power(s) by means of the existence of a public control body. Indeed, Directive 95/46 has extended this control principle across national borders in Article 29, providing for the establishment of a European Working Party, which is in charge of significant tasks and includes representatives from the national supervisory authorities of all member states.

At this point one may actually refer to the "constitutionalization" of individuals in line with the approach followed by the constitutional charters and the decisions of the constitutional courts in many European countries. Privacy is regarded as a fundamental right by the Greek, Spanish, and Portuguese constitutional charters, as well as by the constitutional charters of most Central and East European countries. In its decision of December 15, 1983, the German *Bundesverfassungsgericht* (i.e., the Constitutional Court) recognized that the "right to informational self-determination" was a fundamental right of individuals. Indeed, this approach is followed not only in Europe: for instance, Article 43 of the Argentinean Constitution provides for a *habeas data* principle.

PRIVACY PROTECTION: A SUPRANATIONAL AND INTERNATIONAL PERSPECTIVE

The growing importance attached to the protection of personal data as a fundamental right is producing considerable effects as regards the need for reconciling the interests related to privacy protection with other interests that are also enshrined in constitutional provisions, such as those related to security, health, or "the free flow of personal data between Member States"—the latter being expressly referred to in Article 1(2) of Directive 95/46. Data protection may never be wholly overridden by other interests, albeit of the greatest social importance. Indeed, privacy is a fundamental characteristic of individuals in the information society—a basic component of electronic citizenship.

Based on these premises, a system was set up in the European Union to

- increase the level of personal data protection in the individual member states;

- confer the power to control and develop the operation of this integrated system of personal data protection on supranational bodies, for instance by updating the existing directives or adopting new directives;

- create a geographic and political area where personal data may move freely across the borders of member states; and

- make physical and logical security of data banks a prerequisite for the protection of personal data by providing that member states should take adequate measures to be complied with by any entity processing personal data (see Article 17 of Directive 95/46).

The European system can therefore be regarded as a formal standard based on an international treaty, which envisages multilateral coordination. To ensure common protection, however, it is necessary to regulate not only the relationships between the individual member states, but also those of the EU as a whole with third countries. Otherwise the high level of protection afforded inside the union could easily be overridden by transferring the personal data collected in Europe to data havens (i.e., countries with a definitely lower protection level than the EU).

This entails a concrete cyber-security issue, which has been coped with at the European level by laying down a common protection threshold so that it is irrelevant whether the data are processed in or move to this or that member state. Protection has been therefore shifted from the national to the supranational level. It is now necessary to prevent this result from being nullified by transborder data flows outside the European Union.

In dealing with this issue, Article 25 of Directive 95/46 has set forth the general principle that member states may not allow personal data to be transferred to third countries that do not ensure "an adequate level of protection." The resulting framework is as follows:

- The European Commission may formally decide that the level of protection is adequate. In this case, the data may be freely transferred to the third country whose legislative framework has been considered to be adequate. This has already occurred with respect to Canada, Switzerland, and Hungary. The relevant proceeding is in progress as regards many more countries, including Australia, New Zealand, and Argentina.

- The Commission may conclude a specific agreement with a third country whose legislative framework does not appear to qualify for a general adequacy finding in accordance with European criteria, where the businesses established in that country undertake to adopt specific protection standards. This is the case with the United States and the so-called Safe Harbor Agreement.

- Standard contractual clauses may be instituted to be implemented on a case-by-case basis to ensure adequate protection in connection with a specific data transfer. The European Commission has given a green light to standard clauses allowing personal data to be lawfully transferred to third countries that have not been the subject of a general adequacy finding, or where a business interested in receiving data from EU countries has not adhered to a specific instrument, such as the Safe Harbor for the United States.

- Under Article 26 of the directive there are various derogations allowing data to be transferred to a third country if, for instance, the data subject has given his specific consent or the transfer is necessary on important public interest grounds, for the conclusion or performance of a contract, or for the protection of the vital interests of the data subject.

The above legal framework is an attempt by the European Union to integrate national and supranational levels, the "regional" and the "global" dimension. However, this system obviously cannot cope by itself with all the issues arising from the worldwide movement of personal data. There is the need for a general instrument, such as an international convention on privacy. Indeed, this proposal was put forward in the Venice Declaration, which was approved by the World Conference on Data Protection of 2000 and reaffirmed by the Paris World Conference of 2001. If the new cyber world is global, the regulatory tools must also be global in nature.

Still, despite the existence of a common legal framework, the individual member states of the EU have retained their authority to ensure compliance with the principles enshrined in the directives as transposed into domestic law. Therefore, different approaches have been developed by the national bodies (judiciary, independent authorities) as a function of the peculiar features of national legal systems. However, the attempt has been made by many member states, although on the basis of different technical assumptions, to impose sanctions on the conduct of entities established in third countries where such conduct produces effects inside the EU—as is the case with Web sites that may be accessed from the territory of member states. A French court prohibited the sale of Nazi memorabilia by Yahoo!, which sparked the reaction of a U.S. court rejecting the attempt to impose the laws of another country on the United States in breach of national sovereignty.

This is further proof of the need for definition of one or more international conventions. The applicable law issue should also be taken into account whenever information is collected, processed, and disseminated in nonmember states of the EU.

The latter issue is addressed by Article 4 of Directive 95/46:

"1. Each Member State shall apply the national provisions it adopts pursuant to this Directive to the processing of personal data where:

(a) ....;

(b) the controller is not established on the Member State's territory, but in a place where its national law applies by virtue of international public law;

(c) the controller is not established on the Community territory and, for purposes of processing personal data makes use of equipment, automated or otherwise, situated on the territory of the said Member State, unless such equipment is used only for purposes of transit through the territory of the Community."

Implementation of the above rules sometimes proves rather difficult (what is the meaning of equipment, for instance?), but additional approaches are being developed exactly with a view to meeting the demand for a stepwise definition of common transnational regulations. For instance, in the standard contractual clauses approved by the EU Commission there is the possibility for the contracting parties, in case of disputes, to apply to a panel including representatives from national independent authorities rather than to a national court. This is clearly an attempt to commit dispute resolution to a body operating at a European level, which is accepted by the parties voluntarily and is not set up on the basis of their determinations—as is the case with arbitration proceedings—since it is composed of representatives from national supervisory authorities.

It should also be pointed out that codes of conduct are being used increasingly as a means for developing and supplementing the rules set forth by the EU. These codes are expressly referred to in Article 27 of Directive 95/46 and differ from conventional codes of conduct in that they do not simply reflect sectoral self-regulation. Indeed, they are "certified" by the Working Party set up under Article 29 of the directive, which is entitled to assess their compliance with the principles of the directive. A new source of legal rules is thereby established, in which the regulatory production of private entities is integrated with the assessment performed by public bodies. In this way, codes of conduct can afford the opportunity for setting forth more flexible provisions, which are better suited to sectoral requirements and have increased legal and social force compared with self-regulation.

CIVIL RIGHTS AND CYBER SECURITY

The whole framework of personal data protection in Europe, which is partly the outcome of the integration between the more conventional protection afforded by Council of Europe instruments and the more stringent safeguards laid down by the union, can therefore be said to rest on the following grounds:

- awareness of the need for providing protection based on supranational rules;

- stepwise inclusion of personal data protection rules into the scope of fundamental rights and freedoms, ultimately leading to consideration of data protection as a fundamental right and a basic component of the new citizenship; and

- attempt to reconcile privacy as a value with other values recognized by constitutional principles and society as a whole.

The most significant proof of the need for strong safeguards, which are not related exclusively to the traditional demand for privacy, is given by the specific provisions laid down in Directive 95/46 and, therefore, in domestic laws as regards data concerning racial origin, opinions, health, and sex life. The more stringent protection afforded to these sensitive data is accounted for by the risk that they may be used to discriminate against citizens. A direct link is established in this way between data protection and the equality principle.

On the other hand, the creation of a "European legal area" and the requirements made by the fight against crime and terrorism have made it necessary to have recourse to specific data banks at a European level and to enhance the transnational flows of certain categories of personal data. For instance, establishment of a borderless European area, in which citizens can move freely, has led to collecting information on foreign suspects. Lawfulness of these data banks as provided for by the 1985 Schengen Agreement is conditional upon compliance with the principles included in both Directive 95/46 and Council of Europe Convention No. 108. To ensure that this protection is effective, a supervisory authority has been set up at the European level. This same approach (i.e., data protection plus supervisory authority) has been adopted for matters regulated by the Europol convention (cooperation between law enforcement agencies), the Eurodac convention (collection of fingerprints of applicants for asylum in member states), and the Customs Information System Convention.

As to the fight against crime, the most important instrument is currently the Cybercrime Convention, which was adopted by the Council of Europe in 2001. In particular, this convention includes a number of provisions—see Article 16 and subsequent ones—applying to storage of "specified computer data" and access to these data by judicial and police authorities.

Many sensitive issues have arisen in consequence concerning the need to reconcile data protection with data collection in fighting crime. The latter issue has been repeatedly addressed by the Working Party established under Article 29 of Directive 95/46. Two of the relevant documents are especially significant.

In Recommendation No. 2/99 on the respect of privacy in the context of interception of telecommunications, reference is made to the principles to be abided by to ensure respect for fundamental freedoms. Special importance is attached here to "the prohibition of all large-scale exploratory or general surveillance of telecommunications." This implicitly refers to the Echelon Surveillance System and the resulting problems for the European Union, both because one of its member states (i.e., the United Kingdom) participates in that initiative and because the system is of a transnational nature, which makes it difficult or even impossible to carry out controls in order to safeguard any person whose data are collected.

In Opinion No. 10/2001 on the need for a balanced approach in the fight against terrorism, which was adopted following the September 11 attacks, the Working Party voice their concern for measures that are disproportionate compared with the purpose to be achieved, as well as for unjustified restrictions on the fundamental right to data protection. Reference is made expressly to "the necessity to take into account the long term impact of urgent policies rapidly implemented or envisaged in this moment," and it is concluded that

> [m]easures against terrorism should not and need not reduce standards of protection of fundamental rights, which characterize democratic society. A key element of the fight against terrorism involves ensuring that we preserve the fundamental values that are the basis of our democratic societies and the very values that those advocating the use of violence seek to destroy.

OVERCOMING OBSTACLES TO COOPERATION

THE COUNCIL OF EUROPE
CONVENTION ON CYBERCRIME
James A. Lewis

Faced with the explosive growth and commercialization of the Internet in the 1990s, law enforcement agencies in many countries concluded that their domestic laws were inadequate for a new kind of crime—cyber crime. Someone sitting before a computer in one country could access computer networks in another country to commit crimes in a third country—a "transnational" or "transborder" crime. One study of laws in 52 countries found in 2000 that two-thirds had inadequate cyber-crime laws.[1] Procedures for bilateral law enforcement cooperation, for example, did not always cover computer crimes and were often too slow to be of use.

Cyber crime is part of a larger transnational challenge to law enforcement and the authority of national governments created by the revolution in information technology, easy international travel, and the growth of extensive financial and trade networks. The Council of Europe Convention on Cybercrime defines cyber crime as offenses committed against "the integrity, availability, and confidentiality of computer systems and telecommunication networks" (e.g., the Internet), or the use of networks or their services to commit traditional offenses, including money laundering, offering illegal services, violation of copyright, violations of "human dignity (e.g., racism) and the protection of minors." These challenges can be met only when nations cooperate.

The diplomatic tools developed for the last century for police in one country to request the assistance of police and courts in another—letters rogatory, or Mutual Legal Assistance Treaties (MLATs)—are slow and do not help when national laws are incompatible. Many countries still lack an adequate legal framework for the deterrence and punishment of cyber crimes or rely on an uneven patchwork of legislation. Disagreement over what constitutes a crime, inadequate, uneven, or absent authorities for governments to investigate and prosecute cyber crime; and procedures for international cooperation more attuned to the age of sail than to the Internet have hampered international cooperation on cyber crime.

The transnational aspect of crime is compounded by technological developments that pose new and difficult challenges for law enforcement. Digital evidence is fragile and transitory, and old techniques for wiretapping no longer work. Police agencies in the United States, and elsewhere have felt beleaguered as global forces and new technologies erode their ability to enforce the law.

The U.S. Department of Justice began in the 1990s to work with the Organization for Economic Cooperation and Development (OECD) and the G-8 (Group of 8) to develop cooperative responses to cyber crime. The Council of Europe, which has a mandate to promote the rule of law and human rights, began a similar effort in the late 1980s. In 1995, the council's European Committee on Crime Problems recommended adoption of an international treaty on cyber crime. In February 1997, the Council of Europe created a new committee (the Committee of Experts on Crime in Cyberspace) to prepare a binding convention that addressed computer network offenses, criminal law, and jurisdiction. The United States was invited to be an active participant in the cyber-crime effort along with Japan, Canada, and South Africa. The Committee of Experts maintained a rapid pace, and by December 2000 its drafting group had met 25 times.

At first, this effort attracted little public notice. To its credit, the council made the drafting process unusually open (by diplomatic or business standards. The Committee of Experts released a draft convention to the public, including publication on the Internet (one advantage of the Internet is that it allows texts to be circulated widely for comment—a kind of "open-source" diplomacy) and held a public hearing in March 2001.

The draft tapped a deep reservoir of concern over government intrusiveness and prompted an energetic public response. Corporations and cyber-libertarians found themselves allies in opposing the convention. Twenty-two privacy and business associations in Europe, the United States, Japan, Australia, and South Africa created the "Global Internet Liberty Campaign" to oppose the convention. UNESCO (concerned over the extension of criminal penalties to copyright infringement) and the European Union's Privacy Working Group also offered objections to the draft convention's piracy and data preservation provisions.

The critics' view was that the convention was fundamentally imbalanced, as it provided sweeping powers for computer search and seizure and communications surveillance without corresponding protections for privacy and civil liberties. Information technology groups feared that implementing the convention would be costly. Civil liberties groups stated that the convention could lead to a curtailment of freedom of expression online and gave too many investigative powers to police and government organizations. But entertainment industry groups said that the convention's copyright provisions would help in the battle against crossborder Internet crime.

Business concerns were driven by the potential expense of data-preservation requirements (such as requiring service providers to preserve e-mail routing data). The convention's data-preservation provisions could increase costs and force Internet service providers (ISPs) and other firms to reshape their businesses in ways that were favorable to law enforcement to guarantee surveillance and data recovery. The United States' difficult experience with the "Clipper Chip" and the Communications Assistance to Law Enforcement Act (which requires U.S. telephone companies to build wiretap capacity into their networks) helped prompt this response. The lack of adequate privacy protections for Americans may have also contributed to fears about misuse of data collected by law enforcement. Companies were also concerned that the convention would result in their being liable for criminal acts that crossed their networks.

Early drafts of the convention also contained very broad definitions of criminal conduct that covered a wide range of legitimate behaviors. One section made it an offense to access any computer without permission, effectively if inadvertently criminalizing Web surfing. Similarly, the provisions on illegal devices were drafted to apply to security tools as well as hacking tools.

The extraterritorial application of national laws also raised concerns. Cyberspace may not have any borders, but the computer networks that compose it are physically located in countries and subject to their laws. A signatory to the convention could request assistance in investigating an act that was a crime under its laws but not in the jurisdiction of the nation it was asking for assistance (i.e., an absence of "dual criminality"). Critics said that a dual-criminality provision was "central to preserving the sovereign authority of nations." They called for limitations, clear procedures, and a high level of individual rights protections for international investigations taken under the convention.[2]

The most prominent issue was the provision on police surveillance powers and digital evidence preservation and its implications for privacy. The new technologies have greatly enhanced the ability of governments to intrude on the privacy of their citizens. The Cybercrime Convention was sometimes portrayed as creating Orwellian police powers, and commercial interests echoed these concerns to buttress their opposition to assuming new costs and responsibilities.

There are major differences between U.S. and European attitudes on the role of the state and on privacy. In the United States, the most vocal concerns are over police "wiretapping" of communications, including communication on the Internet. In Europe, there is greater concern over personal data being exploited for commercial use. Many European countries allow their internal security agencies much greater freedom in wiretapping than does the United States. Communications interception has been an essential weapon against crime and terrorism for decades, and the convention only accelerated and formalized the efforts by most countries to extend telephone wiretap capabilities to Internet-based communications.

Another major difference lies in the dissimilarities between Napoleonic law and the United States' approach to common law, with its emphasis on due process and individual rights. Where Europeans sometimes saw U.S. law as inadequate in protecting privacy, European laws did not provide the level of formal protection for civil liberties found in the United States. Bringing Napoleonic and common-law systems into alignment was a fundamental challenge in drafting the convention. If the United States had not participated, the final convention would have looked very different, with a much more Napoleonic (and perhaps draconian) cast.

The final draft was modified substantially to address these concerns (albeit not to the satisfaction of many critics). The convention supplements multilateral and bilateral agreements, harmonizes national laws for cyber crime, and sets the basis for common powers of investigation and "fast and effective" international co-operation. It defines four categories of cyber crime to be covered by signatories' national laws:

- crimes against the confidentiality, integrity, and availability of computer data and systems, including illegal access or interception, interference with data or systems, or misuse of devices;

- computer fraud or forgery;

- content-related crimes. This currently applies to child pornography, but the next step is a protocol covering racist or xenophobic ideas on the Internet, an area of potential conflict for the United States with its free-speech guarantees; and

- intellectual property and copyright infringement crimes, such as the distribution of pirated copies.

One significant change in the final draft was an increased emphasis on rules and safeguards for mutual assistance.[3] Article 15 of the convention now binds signatories, when carrying out these functions, to observe their commitments to the Council of Europe's Convention for the Protection of Human Rights and Fundamental Freedoms and Convention for the Protection of Individuals with Regard to Automatic Processing of Personal Data, as well as to the United Nations' Covenant on Civil and Political Rights.

Language on "intent" was added to ensure that to qualify as criminal, an act must be committed deliberately and "without right." Signatories have also agreed to establish a contact network among Justice ministries to provide immediate investigatory assistance. The convention does not, however, allow police in one country to conduct investigations in another ("transfrontier investigations"). Signatories must cooperate with requests for assistance in collecting computer evidence, but other provisions make clear that countries can refuse to disclose data if they believe this will prejudice their sovereignty, security, or other essential interests, or where they consider the request to be related to a political act. Finally, countries can reserve on sections that are incompatible with their national laws when they sign the convention, and all of the convention's provisions will be reviewed three years after entry into force.

The convention did not include "hate speech" among its cyber crimes, despite a strong desire to do so by many Europeans. The main obstacle to its inclusion was the First Amendment protections given to U.S. Web sites. One expert noted that of the 4,000 or so Internet sites dedicated to hate or racist activities, more than 2,500 are in the United States. Another expert called for European governments to prevent the United States from become a "cyber haven" for racism. One European suggestion was for the United States to deny First Amendment protection to sites whose content is provided in languages not destined for the American public, where content providers are not domiciled in the same country as the ISP, and where visitors are principally based outside of the United States.[4] The Europeans realize that this suggestion is incompatible with the First Amendment and that agreement with the United States is unlikely, but they are moving at a rapid pace to add a protocol to the convention in 2002 to criminalize "acts of racist and xenophobic nature through computer networks" (e.g., production and dissemination of information on the Internet).

This protocol poses serous problems for the United States, not only because of the potential for conflict with the First Amendment. There is also the risk of setting a global precedent for prosecuting U.S. companies when they host content that a country finds offensive.

Many European countries already have this authority (demonstrated by France's prosecution of Yahoo! for hosting Nazi Web sites and by similar cases in Italy and Germany), but the protocol could establish an international legal standard. The United States has little support and less leverage for its stance.

The dispute over the hate-speech protocol should not detract from the benefits of the convention. Although it attracted much criticism during its long negotiation, the Convention on Cybercrime is the most concrete multilateral achievement to date for building better cyber security. It is understandable that better cooperation among police forces can raise fears about privacy and human rights. But the convention allows very different national legal systems to cooperate in investigating and prosecuting cyber crime without yielding their national sovereignty. It does this by creating common definitions of cyber crime and formal processes for cooperation while allowing nations the choice of opting out of specific investigations or provisions.

The Convention on Cybercrime was opened for signature on November 23, 2001. Thirty countries signed it and two of the signing countries (Albania and Croatia) ratified it within a year (five ratifications are required for entry into force). Its rules will apply to most of the world's Internet traffic when it is ratified by the United States, Canada, Japan, and South Africa. Implementing the convention will not be a challenge for the United States, as most of the authorities needed to conform to it are already found in U.S. law.

Preventing unauthorized access to computer systems lies at the core of cyber security and critical infrastructure protection. Effective prosecution of cyber crime can reduce and deter unauthorized access. Cybercrime laws are only part of the solution—cyber security also requires better technology, clearer rules about identity, and mechanisms for coordinated activities and information sharing.

Better security requires many countries to act in a coordinated fashion. Sovereignty—the decision of a group of people to govern themselves without external interference—remains a serious obstacle to cooperation. The Council of Europe Cybercrime Convention is a serious test of the ability of nations to cooperate in Internet security and critical infrastructure protection. The convention revealed substantial differences in national legal systems regarding fundamental issues for cyber space. Although these were successfully bridged in the council's negotiations, for now the Cybercrime Convention may show the limits of the possible in cyber-security cooperation.

Notes

1. "Cyber Crime...and Punishment? Archaic Laws Threaten Global Information," McConnell International, December 2000. www.mcconnell international.com/services/CyberCrime.htm

2. See, for example, the comments of the Global Internet Liberty Campaign letter to the Council of Europe, December 12, 2000; or the comments from the Hearing on Cyber-Crime held by the Parliamentary Assembly of the Council of Europe in Paris on March 6, 2001.

3. Mutual assistance covers such areas as the preservation of stored data; preservation and disclosure of traffic data; production orders; search and seizure of computer data; and real-time collection of traffic data and interception of content.

4. Statement by Beatrice Metraux, of the Swiss Institute of Comparative Law, Council of Europe Hearing on Cyber-crime, March 6, 2001.

CHAPTER NINE

INFORMAL, NON-TREATY-BASED MULTILATERAL COORDINATION

Nobuo Miwa

I believe I was one of the few who originally started the information/network security business in Japan. From early on, I stressed the importance of information and technologies, and I realized the need to take security measures. Today, I am convinced that my beliefs were correct.

The following introduces information on non-treaty-based multilateral coordination, centering on "information and technologies." Although people are more aware than ever of the potential danger of cyber terrorism, there has not been sufficient discussion of its specific hazards or measures to prevent it. In Japan, hardly any measures have been taken against cyber terrorism except by the most farsighted organizations.

Private companies possess security-related technologies and information, but are unlikely to make the concerted effort necessary to form a cooperative system, as their primary concern is the protection of their own business. To combat cyber terrorism and large-scale attacks on information systems, international cooperation is an absolute necessity.

I can offer no simple solutions to the security problems we face, but I will propose policies based on my experience in the security business that I hope will help steer others in the right direction in their security protection efforts.

INTERNATIONAL COORDINATION IN THE INTERNET AGE

The Internet transcends national borders and can even conceal users' identities. In spite of such omnipresence and anonymity, this information network is connected to the networks of large corporations and important social infrastructures. Whenever a computer is connected to an open network, it is exposed to external threats. Cyber criminals are always seeking new security holes, and their methods of attack are becoming increasingly sophisticated. Stalkers, religious cults, and international terrorist groups are increasingly including cyber attacks in their scope of disruptive activities.

Against such a backdrop, we are very interested in learning about actual cases of computer attacks on various companies, and we are eager to identify trends in Internet crimes in other countries.

Unfortunately, sufficient information on the subject is not publicly available. This is only natural, as the companies are reluctant to disclose such information on their vulnerability and degree of damage.

Meanwhile, information on such vulnerability is widely distributed based on the "open source" and "full disclosure" concepts. This practice can have serious effects, however, depending on future trends in the regulation of malicious programs.

As use of the Internet continues to spread, even the elderly and children are now involved in what was formerly the special domain of engineers alone. Together with this, there is the growing notion that information directly involving threats should be concealed, along with our reluctance as a society to discuss the subject of vulnerability.

However, there is no established system or mechanism to predict attacks on computers or networks or to prevent them. Another serious factor is that such attacks can come not only within our own country, but from overseas as well. In addition, it is important to prevent people in our country from attacking the networks of other countries in order to demonstrate that we are an internationally responsible nation.

In view of this situation, I would like to emphasize the importance of governmental support to private companies and organizations possessing advanced security technologies. The government should also establish "Internet-time-adaptive," effective, and long-term measures against cyber terrorism, with the cooperation of neighboring countries.

VIEW ON SECURITY-RELATED INFORMATION

To take security measures, the following general information is required:

- Who attacks what and how?
- What preventive measures can be taken?
- What is the allocated budget and how serious is the commitment?

Unless the method of the attacks is known, it is not possible to take accurate measures to combat attacks. The "difficulty of attack" and "possibility of damage" are closely interrelated. In other words, the possibility of damage suffered by a highly secure system depends on the value of the information contained in that system. If a system is not valuable to computer criminals, there is no need to provide strict protection.

Therefore, the sophistication of an attack must be examined and understood in order to plan effective protective measures. How can one know how resistant a system is to attacks?

To determine the sophistication of an attack, the following conditions must be considered:

- **Presence and extent of security holes (vulnerability).** These include ease of stealing administrator's privilege, and reproducibility under limited conditions.
- **Depths of disclosed information.** The availability of detailed explanations makes it easy to create attack tools.
- **Availability of attack tools.** If attack tools are available, anyone can carry out a computer attack. As attack tools must be modified in most cases for use in actual exploitation attempts, the ease of modification is another important factor.

Collecting the above information requires large amounts of time and effort. Our company collects, processes, and supplies this information. Based on my experience, I consider it more practical for a company to outsource this service than to perform this task in-house.

In implementing actual measures, it is necessary to understand past cases of cyber attacks on and cyber crimes perpetrated in other organizations and foreign countries. Measures must be taken to prevent attacks similar to those that have occurred elsewhere. The World Wide Web operates on its own time, referred to as "Internet time," and this clock does not necessarily correspond to the one used by us. Therefore, the following information must be obtained in order to take security measures.

1. **Information on vulnerability.** To obtain information on security holes in software and hardware, it is necessary to have wide-ranging information resources.

2. **Information on threats.** The acquisition of real-time information on the plans and trends of Internet criminals, new computer viruses, and worms requires international information exchange.

3. **Information on incidents.** The acquisition of information and the analysis of past attacks made on the Internet and intranets also require international information exchange.

4. **Reports.** Documents describing future trends in attacks and threats, security trends in various countries, effective security measures, and the latest security trends are essential for planning proactive security measures.

The following describes our approach for each of the types of information above and the issues remaining to be resolved.

Information on Vulnerability

In the collection of information on vulnerability, such information must ultimately be classified by the technical risk it involves. To that end, generally available information on security holes is collected and scrutinized first in the initial stage of the classification.

This is not sufficient, however, as collected information often contains inaccuracies and is not suitable for our use. Therefore, we must verify the authenticity of distributed information. This requires an extensive testing environment established with a large facility investment.

Technical risks can be classified only after the vulnerability of information is scrutinized and verified.

Issues to be resolved:

- **Growing scarcity of detailed information.** Because detailed information can be used in planning and carrying out cyber attacks, there is a tendency to believe that such information should not be disclosed.

- **Systematic acquisition of information.** The systematic acquisition of information is becoming difficult due to a rapid increase in applications. The number of applications used on the Internet is rising dramatically, and vulnerabilities are increasing accordingly. Obtaining such information requires wide- ranging information sources, including vendor information, as well as a great deal of time and effort.

- **Manufacturers' and producers' cooperation in information disclosure.** Vulnerability information is ultimately gathered by manufacturers and producers. Measures are provided (patching, setting changes, etc.) but, because knowledge of security holes is essential to judge the degree of potential danger, disclosure of information by manufacturers and producers is highly desirable. Nevertheless, most manufacturers and producers refuse to provide detailed information on security holes in their products.

- **Extensive information available on U.S. mailing lists and bulletin boards.** Based on the "full disclosure" policy, mailing lists and bulletin boards in the United States promote the exchange of information for cross-fertilization. Participation in offline communities is also essential, but those in Asia have limited opportunities due to geographical disadvantages.

- **Language problems.** Information on country-specific software is translated into the applicable local languages. Engineers in each country normally exchange information in their native language, so technicians in other countries cannot obtain such information from mailing lists.
- **Lack of standardization of criteria for judging technical risks.** There are no standardized criteria for judging technical risks and exchanging information between countries. The judgment criteria presently vary by engineer.
- **Lack of effort for eliminating vulnerability.**

Information security can be improved dramatically if easy-to-attack security holes are eliminated from major software. However, companies continue to develop software without paying close attention to vulnerability, as manufacturers are not legally responsible for recalling products with security flaws.

Information on Threats

Even if security holes are reported, no cyber attack will occur if there is no available attack tool or method. The judgment of overall risks must be made based on an investigation of attack tools, actual exploitations made in the past, computer viruses and worms spreading on the Internet, and other factors. For attack tools, it is also necessary to check the distribution of tools and subsystems and to examine the ease of their production and modification.

Issues to be resolved:

- **Establishment of a large-scale information-collection mechanism.** As information collection requires an examination of the trends in various countries worldwide, including those in the underworld, private companies cannot collect or analyze sufficient amounts of information single-handedly. Therefore, the recognition and elimination of false alarms and groundless rumors also become important tasks.
- **Cooperation of antivirus software manufacturers.** The cooperation of antivirus software manufacturers is essential for combating computer viruses and worms. Those manufacturers

have worldwide information networks, but disclose only limited information to protect their business interests.

- **Standardization of criteria for judging the ease of attack-tool production.** There are no standardized criteria for judging the ease of developing attack tools. This requires advanced technologies.

- **Standardization of criteria for judging technical risks.** It is difficult to establish criteria for judging overall risks, and there are no commonly used criteria. Time will be required for such criteria to be established.

Information on Incidents

Descriptions and analyses of past incidents provide useful information to companies and organizations. Because Internet crimes occur in various forms and styles, staying abreast of the most recent incidents is very important. It is necessary to learn about individual cases of computer crimes and ongoing incidents caused by computer viruses or worms and by Internet criminal groups.

Issues to be resolved:

- **Definition of computer crime.** The definition of computer crime is ambiguous in countries worldwide, and many cases of Internet crimes are not even remotely connected to cyber terrorism.

- **Absence of damage reports by victims.** Victims of computer attacks tend to conceal the damage out of fear that it will affect their corporate image. Unlike other crimes that occur in the real world, Internet crimes are not reported by third parties or for the purpose of seeking the arrest of perpetrators.

- **Difficulty of gaining a real-time understanding of damage conditions.** Damages caused by intrusion and destruction are difficult to assess immediately. Several months are often required for an investigation to be completed after a computer crime is reported.

- **Dispersion of damage information.** Private network-security companies generally possess information on damages caused by network attacks. When a case is reported to the police, some time is required for the details to be available. In Japan, information is provided to public organizations such as Japan-CERT, but details are not disclosed to the public.

Reports

Obtaining various types of information on a daily basis is necessary. It is also very important to understand security trends. Although it is impossible to thoroughly anticipate future tendencies, it is possible to take measures against foreseeable attacks. Various reports provide information on expected attacks and trends in security measures.

Issues to be resolved:

- **Knowledge of the security industry.** Because information on trends in security measures is transmitted primarily by security-product vendors, it is necessary to be well versed in the industry.

- **Technical knowledge.** Technical knowledge is essential for predicting types of future attacks. The technical levels and purposes of Internet criminals must be forecast based on a thorough knowledge of past attack methods.

- **Information provided by government organizations.** Governmental trends also provide useful information. Information from countries with advanced security technologies, such as the United States, is essential. The collection of such information requires human resources and the appropriate organization.

Common Issues

Various issues related to information collection and analysis have been introduced thus far. A number of those issues are pertinent to each type of information.

- **Securing knowledgeable security engineers.** The tasks of collecting and analyzing information related to computer crimes can be performed only by specialists with more advanced technical expertise and experience than ordinary security engineers. However, there is a shortage of even general security engineers, and it is not considered possible to secure a large number of computer specialists with more advanced security knowledge.

- **Maintaining the skills of individual engineers and providing training.** Security technology constantly advances, and engineers must continue learning new technologies to keep their skills and knowledge up to date. If a sufficient number of engineers could be secured, it would be necessary to provide them with a suitable environment, sufficient time, and a proper training curriculum.

- **Conflicts among private companies.** The exchange of information among private security vendors could affect their own profit structures. Security vendors would like to have information on other vendors, but would not be eager to give out theirs.

- **Deviation between Internet time and government time.** The Internet operates on its own time, referred to as "Internet time," and is designed for user convenience. The government, on the other hand, makes decisions and implements them according to its particular time schedule, referred to as "government time." These two clocks keep completely different times, and the time deviation is an obstacle to the effective implementation of security measures.

PROPOSED SOLUTIONS FOR INDIVIDUAL ISSUES

There are no simple solutions for the aforementioned problems. These problems must be addressed and solved primarily by private security companies and organizations with the full support of the Japanese government, security companies and organizations around the world, and the governments of other countries, all sharing the same goal and awareness and taking coordinated action.

Their mutual trust is also important. It is important to keep in mind that we must abide by the "give and take" principle in information exchange.

The following are the solutions I propose.

1. **Exchange of computer-crime damage information**

   Private security companies have collected a wealth of information, and it is essential to organize and exchange this information. However, as no company wishes to disclose information, it is necessary to design a system that provides benefits to security companies participating in information exchanges, such as the provision of advanced training services, the use of databases, and the acquisition of useful reports.

2. **International exchange of information among engineers on vulnerability and threats**

Information on vulnerability and threats has been entered in databases by private companies, and the government can provide funds and information to help make such databases larger and more thorough and to improve their international usefulness. Such databases do not need to be integrated, but can exist separately in the industry or specific fields. The organizations operating the databases can collaborate internationally to further increase and improve the amount and quality of information.

3. **Limitations on manufacturers' and producers' informa-tion service outlets, and improvement of service quality**

While the disclosure of detailed information on security holes by manufacturers and producers is important, responding to too many inquiries is not desirable, as doing so may increase the risk of malicious exploitation of information. I propose limiting the information service outlets in each country and signing the non-disclosure agreement (NDA) for the disclosure of detailed information on vulnerability.

4. **Development of advanced security-engineer training programs, and long-term implementation on a global scale**

Even the most advanced systems and facilities do not serve any useful function if they are not operated by highly trained security engineers. Fostering advanced security engineers requires superb curriculums and training expertise. There is presently no such training program or curriculum. Existing security training is sufficient for cultivating the skills of "script kiddies" only.

The development of a superb training curriculum requires considerable expense. If the revenues expected to be generated from the sales of training programs justify the investment, interested companies would be attracted to the development of such training programs, although the number of capable companies is very limited. Governmental support is a key in such a project.

5. **Global "honey pot"**

Information being gathered is not satisfactory in terms of quality, and it takes time to respond based on the information. Observing and analyzing actual exploitation incidents will help foster competent security engineers. The observation and analysis of actual attacks and intrusions can be achieved through the use of a "honey pot." The development of a honey pot for use in various countries and for the exchange of information enables the early and effective discovery of Internet crime trends without generating any threats to others. This will also allow the early and effective discovery of new computer worms.

6. **Global intrusion detection systems**

There are many intrusion detection system (IDS) products on the market, but, because they are owned by one company, we cannot expect such products' life and specification requirements to meet our specific needs.

We can improve technical levels significantly by developing our original products with the most suitable specifications and functions, and incorporating purposeful activities such as research into uses of signatures and the exchange of information. The development of use of signatures as a means of countering cyber terrorism should be initiated as soon as possible.

7. **Proactive vulnerability discovery activities**

Collecting information on vulnerability alone does not allow us to make preemptive strikes against hackers. Nor does it enable us to exceed the technical levels of cyber attackers. Promoting the active discovery and correction of security holes in major products can help cultivate capable engineers and prevent worms.

8. **Technical guidance to manufacturers and producers for the reduction of vulnerability**

The discovery and correction of security holes are never-ending tasks, but measures must be taken to prevent manufacturers and producers from creating products without giving sufficient consideration to security issues. Acquiring the skill necessary to develop vulnerability-free systems requires a large investment. The government can provide effective assistance by offering training support and subsidies for the development of high-integrity systems.

9. **Standardization of criteria for judging the degree of vulnerability and the potential risk**

Some of the standardizations mentioned above may require an unrealistically long time for establishment if an agreement must be reached through discussion. The most efficient means of establishing standards is to publish standards that will be observed and will become de facto standards.

Government's Role in the Operations of Private Companies

Some people insist that a neutral organization is essential for accomplishing the aforementioned objectives, but no company will send its highly capable employees to an external organization. We must realize that we observe Internet time and must come to terms with the fact that companies will not release their excellent human resources to an external organization. I propose that the government selects and supports companies with superb engineers, high morale, and good results.

When the selected companies or company groups share information with overseas private organizations, it will be possible to cultivate and secure superb engineers.

The most appropriate form of governmental involvement in ensuring cyber security is support of the private sector: private companies are the constant targets of cyber attacks that are always evolving, and these companies must continually develop new security measures to combat them.

Therefore, governments worldwide should create an international environment that allows selected companies and company groups to operate easily on a global scale. For example, the following activities can achieve the intended result:

- holding international conferences;

- providing financial support to selected companies and company groups;

- implementing governmental negotiation and coordination to promote collaboration among selected companies and company groups in individual countries;

- bridging the technical and information gaps among companies and company groups selected in individual countries;

- certifying advanced security engineers and establishing preferential systems; and

- legally restricting the distribution of false program information

Establishment of Research Organizations Dedicated to Cyber Terrorism Prevention

Due to the problem of securing security engineers and the time factor, I have stressed the importance of utilizing private companies for the effective design of security measures. This solution model, however, cannot solve the problem of cyber terrorism perpetrated against key infrastructures.

The anti-cyber terrorism business is a niche market for security-service vendors. However, the prevention of cyber terrorism requires exploitation forecasting and attack defense technologies of much higher levels than those for general worms and Internet crimes. It also involves the issue of national defense in terms of protecting the confidentiality of research activities.

As such, not all activities should be conducted only by private companies; organizations dedicated to research on cyber terrorism should be founded. However, due to the possibility that established organizations may not have appropriate engineers as staff members, it is necessary to consider taking certain drastic measures, such as acquiring security research organizations.

At any rate, international coordination efforts must be led by governments, and national defense-level confidentiality must be maintained.

CHAPTER TEN

BRINGING INTERNATIONAL GOVERNANCE TO CYBER SPACE

John J. Hamre, Prakash Ambegaonkar,
and Katherine Crotty Zuback

No problem so typifies the challenges of governance in the twenty-first century as cyber security. Governing cyber space is both familiar and foreign to national governments. During the past decade, governments have gradually developed approaches to extend sovereign control over cyber space. The state of government control around the world is uneven, but advancing quickly. Traditional concepts of private property, theft, fraud, misrepresentation, value—all concepts rooted in the physical world back to the very earliest manifestations of "law"—are now being extended to the virtual world. Governments are extending statutory social objectives—restricting the sale of unacceptable materials, for example—to cyber space. Governments around the world are increasingly familiar with cyber activities and willing to extend legal control over them. As such, governing cyber space is familiar territory.

Yet cyber space is also alien terrain. No other form of social interaction so quickly transcends national borders and outruns sovereign reach. Activity perfectly legal in one country yet illegal in the next cannot be easily blocked at a border. Indeed, what constitutes a cyber border is yet to be conclusively determined. The borderless quality of cyber space has exacerbated national differences in social policy. Where the sale of Nazi memorabilia is protected as a "freedom of speech" right in the United States, such sales are explicitly illegal in France. Sovereign controls that work for the physical world are strained when extended to the virtual world.

The need for transnational governance is well established. Examples abound of undesirable activities effected by persons in one sovereign state against persons and/or assets in other states.[1] More and more, these activities are taking place in three or more countries. The frequency of undesirable activities (e.g., Web defacements, denial of service, stealing of private information, and more) is rising and includes activities driven by politics, economics, private satisfaction, and personal gain. But not all states have enacted laws to deal with such activities.

Some attacks are without malicious intent and are conducted perhaps for self-satisfaction. Nonetheless, they usually present a hazard to the public. For example, a juvenile hacker disabled a key telephone company computer that serviced the Worcester airport control tower, thereby disabling the main radio transmitter as well as a circuit that enabled approaching aircraft to send signals activating the runway lights. The young hacker also disabled a telephone network in Rutland, Massachusetts, and accessed and downloaded information from a pharmacist's computer. In addition to significant financial damages, his actions threatened public health and safety and personal privacy rights.[2]

Other attacks reflect desires for political and/or economic gains. Perhaps the most notorious cyber attacks are those relating to the Al Qaeda attack on the world trade centers. Vigilante groups like the Rev and a group calling itself the Dispatchers made calls for attacks on perceived terrorist sites. Confirmed cyber attacks include an attack by Fluffi Bunni,[3] a habitual Web site defacer, who modified a specific domain name system server, thus redirecting thousands of site visitors to another page that declared "Fluffi Bunni goes JIHAD." In another site defacement, Fluffi Bunni included the message, "If you want to see the Internet again, give us Mr. Bin Laden and $5 million in a brown paper bag. Love, Fluffi B." Other high-profile groups jumping into the counterterrorism effort include: G-Force Pakistan and Kim Schmitz and his YIHAT organization (Young Intelligence Hackers Against Terrorism).

Relatively few of the individuals responsible for these activities are brought to justice, although the numbers are increasing as more governments enact the necessary laws and participate in international investigations. For example, in 2000, the Philippine government had to drop all charges against "Love Bug" suspect Onel de Guzman because at the time the government did not have an applicable cyber-crime law—despite estimates of up to $10 billion in damages.

Multiple methods are available for transnational governance. Countries enter into treaties or join international organizations that stipulate explicit rules of procedure for resolving conflicting interests. In addition, other, less rigid methods of transnational governance have evolved. Countries join international institutions that stipulate "standards" for activities or performance. Also, countries establish informal working ties—liaison arrangements between customs organizations, for example—to work through shared bilateral problems.

How will international governance for cyber space develop? What patterns are most likely to work? What problems are inherently susceptible to international solution and what problems will resist it? To answer these questions, we should first define the required functions for control over cyber space.

SOVEREIGN CONTROL OF CYBER SPACE

Transnational governance of cyber space cannot differ from transnational governance of any other activity. Governments need first to establish effective sovereign control over their territory, and from that national basis establish cooperation with other partner countries that share a common interest in regulating the activities. During the past five years there has been enormous progress in bringing sovereign control over cyber space. While mechanical details vary widely from country to country, effective sovereign control is built around eight basic functions:

- codification of illegal acts in cyber space;
- legal authority to investigate potential wrongdoing;
- legal authority to compel changes on private activities;
- legal authority to regulate products and service providers;

- coordination mechanisms for government deliberation;
- liaison mechanisms for public/private interaction;
- forensics capabilities to support investigations; and
- adjudication mechanisms (legal and/or administrative) to resolve conflicting interests in the private sector.

There are many different examples to illustrate these functions. We will refer to the experience in the United States to illustrate our arguments. We are not recommending that the American experience is the only, or even the best, way to establish sovereign control in these areas.

Legal Framework

It has proved relatively easy to establish legal authorities and adjudication mechanisms, primarily by extending to the virtual world legal concepts written to govern physical activities. Legal authorities governing cyber service providers, for example, represented only a modest extension from existing legal authorities governing telecommunication entities.

In 1991, the U. S. Department of Justice established a special unit, now known as the Computer Crime and Intellectual Property Section (CCIPS)[4] to guide the department's initiatives to define cyber crimes and to establish guidelines for law enforcement organizations and states attorneys in pursuing potential legal action. Today, CCIPS has a leading role in many cyber-crime investigations. It also performs coordination and technical support roles in many national investigations—supporting investigators and prosecutors dealing with emerging information technologies and crime. In addition to operational activities, CCIPS also serves as chair of the National Cybercrime Training Partnership (NCTP). This partnership provides a forum for 173 organizations[5] to share subject matter expertise for multiple types of law enforcement personnel and to participate in integrated training programs. CCIPS is also recognized as an authoritative source for review and analysis of legislative and policy activities. Through its efforts, CCIPS has demonstrated remarkable success in combating cyber crime on both a national and international scale.[6]

CCIPS understood early the importance of international cooperation, and the section has devoted considerable time and effort to working with international organizations such as the Group of Eight (G–8) Subgroup on High-Tech Crime, which CCIPS chairs. The section has also worked very closely with the Council of Europe on the Convention on Cybercrime. The Council began work on the treaty in 1993, and the section worked with the treaty drafters to establish a treaty acceptable to the United States. The United States formally initialed the treaty on November 23, 2001, and the State Department plans to submit it to the U.S. Senate for consideration and ratification. This initiative has now established a common framework among the 32 signatory countries[7] to define what constitutes illegal activity in cyber space. In addition to a common framework, the treaty establishes a standardized set of operational procedures to guide intergovernmental coordination on transnational cyber crime cases.

At the same time that legal definitions of crime and legal authorities have been established, areas remain—for example, regulatory areas—where the legal basis of control in the United States is still evolving. The basis for taxing transactions in cyber space is still unsettled. A patchwork of regulation currently governs the government's review of products. For example, export controls effectively govern the sale of encryption software, even though there are no restrictions on the sale of encryption products inside the United States. Restrictions on the computer processing speed of exports continue to threaten sale of products. The government has tended to rely on industry-based standards development for regulating the introduction of new products.

In short, while there has been substantial advance in cyber sovereignty in recent years, a considerable range of issues are yet to be resolved and solutions to be developed. The foregoing discussion addresses the first four components of cyber sovereignty noted above. The last component, adjudication mechanisms, has also been covered by extension of the existing mechanisms. As is usually the case, it is easier to establish the legal framework for government action than it is to build the actual infrastructure required to implement it. There has been less progress on the development of a government infrastructure to support these authorities.

Interagency Coordination

To promote interagency coordination, the Clinton administration created a National Infrastructure Protection Center in 1998 housed in the Department of Justice. The NIPC was designed to provide a focal point for receiving information on emerging cyber disruption problems and to coordinate the federal government's response. The NIPC was actually the second attempt to create this capability. The first effort—the Infrastructure Protection Task Force—was widely considered a failure because bureaucratic forces inside the Justice Department and the Federal Bureau of Investigation prevented other organizations from joining it and prevented the organization itself from addressing cyber crime problems in the Bureau. The NIPC, however, has improved its coordination efforts. The center is staffed by a variety of armed services personnel and a dozen federal agencies, as well as representatives from the United Kingdom, Canada, and Australia. In addition, the NIPC has established information-sharing connectivity with a number of foreign cyber watch centers, including the UK, Canada, Australia, New Zealand, and Sweden.

There continues to be considerable disagreement about the effectiveness of the NIPC. Critics charge that the NIPC has become captured by the traditional operational philosophy of the FBI, which pursues investigations along traditional lines ill suited to the fast-changing nature of cyber crime and cyber disruption. More significantly, there is considerable debate within the cyber security community about the task of the NIPC—whether it is to support the development of a legal case that could be made against violators or, rather, whether its task is to quickly diagnose and insulate America's infrastructure from further disruption, even though that arguably would jeopardize the prospects for building a case that can be litigated successfully. Lately, the NIPC, Congress, and industry appear to be reaching agreement on key concerns—most important, the concern that "private" information may be released to competitors through the Freedom of Information Act.[8] In addition to procedural protection measures being developed among the NIPC and industry, the U.S. Congress is considering legislation that explicitly exempts such information from the Freedom of Information Act.

Public-Private Coordination

More by accident than by central policy direction, the United States has developed an effective network of emergency response centers as the primary interface between the government and the private sector. The first major computer emergency response center was established at Carnegie-Mellon University as a derivative activity of the federally funded Software Engineering Institute. Although funded initially by the Defense Department, the Computer Emergency Response Team Coordination Center (CERT/CC) operated independently and has been seen as a private-sector initiative—despite growing links with the NIPC. A major success for this DOD initiative is the use of the CERT/CC as a model for other CERTs created worldwide. Later, the CERT/CC and others established the Forum of Incident Response and Security Teams (FIRST),[9] an international organization that links independent CERTs worldwide. There is no effort to "regulate" these CERTS, one of the key reasons for their success, we believe.

The other major effort at public-private liaison—the development of sector-specific mechanisms for reporting problems to the government—has been less successful. Most of the sector liaison mechanisms have been set up along formal government regulatory lines.[10] For instance, the Department of Energy (DOE) asked the North American Electric Reliability Council (NERC) to serve as the sector coordinator for the electric industry sector. They have since established an information sharing and analysis center, which provides for voluntary incident reporting and is linked to the NIPC. To date, private-sector entities have been reluctant to report cyber problems to their regulatory oversight agencies. They have feared that such reports would trigger oversight investigations and the problems could be disclosed, creating public relations problems for the victim company. This reticence is changing, however, as cyber disruption grows as a problem and company victimization carries less of a stigma of management competence. Indeed, in recent months, the NIPC has greatly increased the interaction with Information Sharing and Analysis Centers (ISACs) representing the different sectors, building on their success with the DOE/NERC experience.

Cyber Forensics

Computer forensics capabilities have developed in both the private sector and government channels. The bulk of forensics capabilities are found in the IT industry itself. Unfortunately, we have become all too accustomed to company alerts of problems and the development of software "patches" to correct identified shortcomings. The government is also creating robust cyber forensics capabilities, and is challenged by the increasing complexity and speed of new generation information technologies. To maintain pace with these changes, the Defense Department law enforcement offices have collaborated to establish the DOD Computer Forensics Laboratory (DCFL), and the FBI is building on this capability—and other national and international efforts—for its own investigation needs. The U.S. government has also entered into contracts with profit-seeking and nonprofit research institutes for cyber forensics services.

Other Programs of Sovereign Control of Cyber Space

Beyond these fundamental attributes of sovereign control, we can expect to see several important related, but less essential, features of sovereign control emerge in coming years. Governments are likely to develop or encourage some method for "professionalizing" cyber personnel. Most modern societies have established procedures for determining the competence of professional service providers, be they accountants, doctors, real estate agents, or financial managers. In some instances, the government operates a formal credentialing process, such as for the licensing of doctors. In other instances, the government either explicitly or tacitly endorses an industry-led credentialing procedure, as in the case of accountants. In the area of cyber security, both industry and government have begun establishing some standards.[11]

MODELS OF TRANSNATIONAL GOVERNANCE

Developing the generic attributes of sovereign control discussed above is the necessary first step and precondition for any system of global governance. The shared vulnerability to unregulated cyber space brings peril to all countries. It is one of the important ironies of our time that the second most important step a country can take to protect its domestic enterprises and citizens, after establishing strong tools for sovereign control over cyber space at home, is to help other governments establish equally strong sovereign control methods over their respective national entities.

Domestic control constitutes a necessary but insufficient condition for transnational governance of cyber space. Intergovernmental collaboration becomes essential. In a world of sovereign states, the evolution toward transnational governance is uneven and multidimensional. There are numerous global governance models that operate with varying degrees of effectiveness and efficiency. We believe it is useful to array these models for purposes of this discussion along two axes—formality and scope.

Formality

Formality refers to the codification of rules and penalties associated with transnational governance and behavior. Such rules may be stipulated in treaties and agreements, at one extreme, or simply outlined as informal operating procedures at the other. Formality does not equate to effectiveness. The League of Nations was elaborately formal, yet entirely ineffective. The informal collaboration of the United States and Canadian customs organizations is enormously effective, and could never be matched in effectiveness by a formal, treaty-based collaboration outlined between, say, the United States and China. Informal collaboration between national police entities can often far outpace the formal authorities outlined in legal agreements. It would be a serious mistake to confuse effectiveness with formality.

At the same time, certain government functions can never be handled informally. Most governments, and especially representative democracies, embody due process protections in government procedures. For example, no country will turn over a cyber criminal to another country without having extradition procedures in place that are consistent with their domestic legal environment. Constitutional democracies are essentially based on the rule of law and a series of explicit procedures that insure due process. Such procedures are essentially formal in nature, and transnational collaboration on cyber crime must necessarily also be formalized. Domestic legal procedures, grounded in unique national experiences and cultural customs, are rarely uniform.

Moreover, informal collaboration, while effective in managing immediate problems, does not significantly contribute to the development of broader environmental conditions that shape the evolution of policy and practice. An informal collaboration between two countries does not easily become an international norm for behavior.

Scope

Scope refers to the number of entities involved in a transnational governance mechanism. We have many examples to study. Obviously, at one extreme is the United Nations with 189 member states and a highly elaborate secretariat and infrastructure. At the other end of the spectrum are the far more common and numerous bilateral ties between two countries. Again, size (in this instance, presumably, inversely to size) does not ensure effectiveness; the wider the scope of intergovernmental coordination, the greater the difficulty and the more complex the administrative burdens to support the arrangement.

Large, complex, multilateral governance mechanisms, however, become more institutionalized in the operation of member countries. As such, formal, multilateral associations have a greater role in creating broad environmental values and norms of behavior among member states over time. A bilateral legal convention between two countries will rarely become the subject of classes in law schools, whereas almost every law school devotes some time to the principles of international law as practiced in the Hague, for example.

COMPLICATIONS FOR TRANSNATIONAL GOVERNANCE

Before outlining a potential strategy for evolving toward more effective transnational governance of cyber space, we should note several issues that complicate the prospect for transnational governance.

Interagency Coordination

Working with foreigners comes easier than working with colleagues. It is an intriguing phenomenon that, in general, collaboration between like agencies in two different countries is often more effective than coordination between two agencies within the same country. The U.S. Customs Service, for example, operates very effectively with customs organizations in other countries, but has in the past not worked well with the U.S. Justice Department and the U.S. Immigration and Naturalization Service. The Central Intelligence Agency has intimate working ties with intelligence services in other countries, but (at least until recent years) chilly and contentious relations with the Federal Bureau of Investigation.

This ironic situation is a byproduct of normal bureaucratic politics. Domestic agencies compete with each other for budget resources. Cooperation with international counterparts, by contrast, enlarges an agency's effectiveness and enhances its competitiveness for resources inside the government when compared to other departments. In the American setting, there are more than a dozen federal law enforcement agencies and they all compete fiercely against each other for mission and resources.

During the past two decades, we have seen an explosion of collaborations between U.S. departments and agencies and their counterparts in other countries. In some of our larger embassies, nearly half of U.S. government personnel accredited to the embassy are not employees of the State Department but liaison representatives from other departments and bureaus of the U.S. government. Many departments have established formalized attaché representatives with major partner countries.

This basic feature of bureaucratic politics is arguably the largest barrier to improved transnational governance of cyber security. Controlling organizational information and data constitutes one of the basic attributes of organizational behavior. When establishing liaison arrangements with parallel institutions in other countries, agencies develop specific procedures and guidelines for sharing information. In almost every instance, those procedures preclude the distribution of that information beyond the receiving bureau, primarily because it is difficult to understand how information may be retransmitted within another country. This is a thoroughly logical restriction, but it also reinforces the bureaucratic parochialism that plagues twenty-first-century government operations. Effective transnational governance of cyber space must confront this central reality.

Industry and Government Perspectives

Industry perception of cyber space governance differs from that of governments. Perhaps governments—the U.S. government in particular—are the cause of this problem. Government began the call for cyber security by focusing on something they termed "cyber warfare." Industry generally does not buy into such a model. Instead, they focus on a financial model that weighs investment costs to potential earnings—and such a model, until recently, did not recognize returns from investments in security features. That is no longer the case. Leaders from many companies (CISCO, Microsoft, Oracle, to name just a few) now recognize that to achieve their business goals, security is no longer an optional investment.[12] Despite this progress, governments still need to overcome the origins of the problem, which lie in the different paradigms faced by government and business, and their differing approaches to resolving the often-competing interests of privacy, business, and public safety. This is very important, as the solutions to preventing and responding to cyber crime will depend on both government and non-government actors.

The Internet

Government no longer "owns" the Internet. This is identified as a complication only in that more than 85 percent[13] of the critical infrastructure is owned by the private sector, and the routing of data across the infrastructure may automatically entail routing through assets located in different countries. Accordingly, governments will find it difficult, if not impossible, to independently affect the operations of cyber space without the coordinated efforts of other nations and industry. Accordingly, governance of this activity must include a high degree of cooperation, not only with other governments but also with international industry. There are situations in other fields (e.g., clear air activities) that drive similar partnerships, but none are as tightly integrated with an underlying industrial base.

EVOLVING EFFECTIVE TRANSNATIONAL GOVERNANCE OF CYBER SPACE

We begin with two propositions. First, effective transnational governance of cyber space will by necessity have features of formality and informality, and of varying scope. We have two simultaneous challenges. The first is to get something done, which invariably begins with informal, bilateral arrangements, and second to establish broad international norms of conduct, which essentially requires formal, multilateral instruments. Second, we are not beginning with a clean slate. We have the opportunity to build on existing patterns and associations, accepting the distortion that comes from structures established at an earlier time to address a different circumstance. Nonetheless, we recommend five steps that would advance the cause of effective transnational cyber space governance.

Semiannual Legal Framework Conferences

The Council of Europe treaty establishes a foundation for harmonizing legal frameworks internationally for cyber protection. Even the strongest proponents of the treaty, however, acknowledge that the treaty at this stage is little more than a multilateralization of the web of bilateral legal assistance agreements or treaties that have been in place for years. The Council of Europe process calls for periodic consultation of the signatory parties, as appropriate, to facilitate discussion on the effective use and implementation of the Convention, to provide a forum for the exchange of information on significant factors (legal, policy, technological developments), and to discuss possible supplements or amendments to the Convention. We believe that the process should establish a formal coordination conference every six months and should establish a specific process for preparing new countries for joining the treaty. We believe that an informal collaboration conference is especially feasible among the five participating governments of the Singapore Cyber Security Conference (Australia, Hong Kong, Japan, Singapore, and the United States), given their shared interest in cyber security and the need to work through operational aspects of their collective tasks.

The more important aspect of the semiannual conferences is to identify and resolve emerging operational issues. Actual cases invariably divulge new requirements for operating procedures. A regular process for implementation review conferences would advance the development of effective new procedures. We also note that overwhelmingly the participants in the Council proceedings are members of the law enforcement community. This effective transnational community collaboration breaks down when brought back to the member countries. We believe that signatory countries should intentionally expand the nation delegation process to widen agency participation. A multiagency meeting of the five Singapore Conference governments would be an excellent starting point for this process.

The semiannual conference should also include continuing discussions on the future governance model for cyber space. The focus of this conference, and of the Council of Europe treaty, is on cyber crime. However, the governance of cyber space involves numerous international aspects, including technical standards and architectural issues. The activities of the conference must include ongoing assessments to ensure current actions do not drive future decisions by default. For example, the future may entail a more formalized governance structure for all cyber space issues, such as that envisioned by Seymour Goodman [chap. 6]. Actions taken in the near term by conference participants should not unduly restrict options for future governance models. Therefore, conference participants must continuously review current activities and update their vision of their future governance model.

Rules and Procedures for Sharing Information

As noted above, the greatest operational impediments to transnational governance are the information-sharing restrictions that generally are imposed in agency-to-agency collaboration agreements. The framework of information sharing will essentially build on agency-to-agency data sharing. Until this problem is fixed, there will be only halting progress toward more effective governance.

New procedures or operational rules are needed to permit wider sharing of information. These could develop along the lines used for sharing classified information in a formal alliance, such as NATO, for example. Alternatively, information could be buffered by an intermediate organization that removes "sources and methods" indicators that might compromise an ongoing investigation, for example.

We do not believe that ground rules can be developed by outsiders or in abstract terms. We believe that this essentially must involve the work of government delegations. We suggest that a small group of countries charter themselves to develop operational rules for sharing information and build upon efforts like the Points of Contact Network, which provides a network of experts who are available 24 hours a day, seven days a week, to assist in high-tech crime investigations.[14]

Joint Infrastructure Protection Coordination Center

Each country is finding appropriate ways to monitor cyber space domestically and to alert private sector infrastructure owners and providers of emerging problems. We believe a more predictable way is needed for surveillance and warning information in one country to be shared with partner countries. We believe that a useful analogue for this activity is found in the United States with the National Strategic Telecommunications Advisory Committee, or NSTAC.[15] Under the auspices of the NSTAC, telecommunications companies send representatives to work at a center maintained by the Department of Defense as executive agent for the U.S. government. This standing liaison organization permits the rapid review of technical data in a manner that preserves the privacy requirements of individual companies while permitting the sharing of emerging threat information. The center also permits coordination in anticipation of scheduled events that could put operational demands on the telecommunications system. While DOD serves an executive agent, the members of the center are mainly industry leaders in telecommunications and information technology experts. The center provides a nonattribution forum that encourages free exchange of ideas and concerns.

We believe that signatory countries should establish a joint infrastructure coordination center along the same guidelines as the NSTAC. The purpose of the coordination center would be to host liaison representatives from both government and private-sector entities to monitor and react to technical developments in the international and domestic cyber networks.

We would expect this center to establish links for information sharing to organizations such as the ISAC and CERT organizations described earlier. Like the ISAC and CERT, this organization would have the ability to provide advance notification of issues, but on an international scale. The center would also have the ability to promote awareness of the risks of lax security in cyber space—an issue raised repeatedly during the Cyber Security Conference. Of particular importance, this organization could drive efforts to better understand the interdependences of the infrastructure and business/government processes, an issue identified by many conference participants as a major deficiency to understanding the vulnerabilities of the cyber world.

Joint Forensics Center

As noted above, computer forensics capabilities are located in both government and private hands. There is, at present, no predictable way to ask forensics questions across government lines. Interpol has created regional working parties in order to leverage the expertise of experts worldwide. These working parties are still under development, but provide an opportunity for member states to share experiences and expertise. They also provide a forum through which world-class expertise can be applied anywhere in the world—through direct or educational services.

We believe this international organization can be used as a basis for establishing a small forensics center that would act as a clearinghouse for questions that emerge in individual countries. The forensics center would not undertake forensics activity directly, but instead maintain awareness of forensics capabilities in partner countries and in private-sector entities. By this we mean that the center would not focus on individual police-type forensic efforts but, rather, would establish the broader policy guidelines and structure to ensure the ability to conduct coordinated investigations.

This forensics center could also emerge as the primary international node for the informal network of the international 24/7 network of experts referenced earlier. In addition, the center could coordinate international training efforts. Training across international boundaries is an essential element to successful investigations into cyber crime. Under most current procedures, investigation within a state is performed by that state. Accordingly, a government that believes data may be located in another government must work through that government to obtain the information. This makes the originating government heavily dependent on the skills and abilities of others to conduct investigations on their behalf. Weak training in any one country may have the same effect as lax cyber crime laws—the creation of a cyber crime haven.

Coordinating Research and Development Initiatives

Currently, some information sharing takes place between governments and private organizations about research and development initiatives. Governments occasionally provide lists of research areas to the private sector to promote greater investments in those areas. More rarely, private industry provides a peek into their research directions. Usually, industry is reluctant to share such information before they are positioned to capture their market share. However, global governance of cyber crime, and cyber space, requires an understanding of the evolution of new technology. We need to find a balance that allows those providing governance functions to prepare for the future, yet protect the financial investments and future earnings of the businesses developing those future technologies.

We propose that a forum be established to provide an opportunity for industry, governments, and other interested parties to review the state of technology and near- and long-term research initiatives. Such a forum could be sponsored by the Joint Infrastructure Protection Coordination Center (proposed above), or under the auspices of the Council of Europe cyber crime convention (initially). The center may be most appropriate in the short term, given its all-encompassing oversight of cyber space. In addition, the limited membership and interaction rules should encourage increased sharing of information.

SUMMARY

The steps outlined above might seem like modest ones, but they represent useful operational advances that can constitute the basis for more formal structures over time. All of the recommendations share a common philosophy. They build on existing, functional informal arrangements, yet they have the potential to grow toward formal, norm-setting institutions over time. As noted above, governing cyber space cannot differ from the basic requirements or principles that govern the sovereign control of physical reality. We must both strengthen sovereign control at home and knit together governments through effective liaison arrangements. The progress toward transnational governance has been remarkably speedy. But we are just at the early stages of this needed development. Modest, practical first steps are all that can, and arguably all that should, be attempted at this time. But these must be steps designed to meet a strategic purpose.

The five governments represented at the March 2002 Cyber Security Conference can serve as major sponsors of these steps, leading by demonstration. They cannot, however, satisfy the objectives without near universal participation of all governments. National boundaries are no longer sacrosanct. The issues of cyber crime— and cyber space—demand participation by all governments. To accept anything less would be, by default, to authorize the creation of cyber havens, or "free rides," or both, for nonparticipating entities. Although 100 percent participation is unlikely, it must remain the goal.

Notes

1. For specific examples, see Web pages posted by the U.S. National Infrastructure Protection Center (www.nipc.gov/warnings/warnings.htm) and the Computer Crime and Intellectual Property Section of the U.S. Department of Justice (www.usdoj.gov/criminal/cybercrime/cybercrime.html). Hacking groups and nonprofit organizations also post examples (e.g., see the Attrition.org pages, which include mirrors of hacked pages, and www.meib.org/articles/0011_ip2.htm, which presents an article from the Middle East Intelligence Bulletin detailing denial of service and Web defacement attacks).

2. See www.usdoj.gov/criminal/cybercrime/juvenilepld.htm

3. The attacker(s), known as "Fluffi Bunni," varies the spelling of his/her name (e.g., Fluffy Bunny).

4. CCIPS began as the Computer Crime Unit of the former General Litigation and Legal Advice Section of DOJ's Criminal Division in 1991. CCIPS became a section of the Criminal Division in 1996.

5. As of January 17, 2002, the partnership included 88 state and local entities, 34 federal agencies, 15 academia groups, 20 private organizations, and 16 international organizations.

6. For press releases of recent cyber crime activities, go to http://www.usdoj.gov/criminal/ cybercrime/.

7. Including four nonmember states: Canada, Japan, South Africa, and the United States.

8. See www.usdoj.gov/04foia/foiastat.htm

9. The Forum of Incident Response and Security Teams was created to resolve perceived difficulties that were encountered between teams during the "Wank Worm" incident. This organization has more than 100 registered teams (CERT, SIRT, etc.) worldwide.

10. In 1998, the president assigned liaison accountability to specified agencies for each infrastructure sector that could be a target for significant cyber or physical attacks. He also strongly encouraged the creation of private-sector Information Sharing and Analysis Centers (ISACs) for the following areas: Information and Communications, Banking and Finance, Water Supply, Transportation, Emergency Law Enforcement Services, Emergency Fire Service and Continuity of Government Services, Public Health Services, and Electric Power and Oil and Gas Production/Storage.

11. Cyber-security experts are few but in high demand, and educational institutions are stepping in to fill the void. Learning institutions are creating graduate programs in computing security; professional societies are creating formalized certification programs; and the National Security Agency has desig-

nated 23 universities as "Centers of Academic Excellence in Information Assurance" using criteria based on training standards established by the National Security Telecommunications and Information Systems Security Committee (NSTISSC).

12. Paul Kurtz , senior director for National Security, Critical Infrastructure Protection, National Security Council, speaking at March 2002 Joint Conference on Cyber Security, hosted by IDSS (www.ntu.edu.sg/idss/) and CSIS (www.csis.org). Participants included government representatives from Australia, Hong Kong, Japan, Singapore, and the United States.

13. Percentage cited is a generally accepted low-end estimate.

14. The Network is the result of an action plan created by the G-8's Subgroup on High-Tech Crime. This subgroup, which was created by the G-8's Senior Expert Group on Transnational Organized Crime (also known as the "Lyon Group"), developed 10 principles and a 10-point action plan to combat high-tech crime. These were adopted by the G-8's Justice and Interior ministers in Washington, D.C., in December 1997. The action plan specifically called for the establishment of a network of designated points of contact, available seven days a week, 24 hours a day, from each member country to assure effective response to transnational high-tech cases. The network has since been expanded from the G-8 to include several additional countries around the world.

15. See www.ncs.gov/nstac/nstac.htm

INDEX

Page numbers followed by the letter n refer to notes.

CCB. *See* Commercial Crime Bureau

CCC. *See* Cybercrime Convention

CCIPS. *See* Computer Crime and Intellectual Property Security

Central Intelligence Agency (CIA): cyber crime offenses, 19

CERT/CC. *See* Computer Emergency Response Team Coordination Center

Charter of Fundamental Rights, 81–82

Chase Manhattan Bank, 39, 40

CISCO, 123

Citibank, 31

civil aviation, 78n

civil rights, 72–73, 92

Clinton administration, 117

"Clipper Chip," 92

Cloverdale, California, 6

CNN, 6, 31

Code Red, 10n

Commercial Crime Bureau (CCB): and Internet fraud, 40–41

Communications Assistance to Law Enforcement Act, 92

Computer Crime and Intellectual Property Security (CCIPS), 115–116

Computer Crime and Security Survey, 2001, 1

Computer Emergency Response Team (CERT), xx, 75, 126; cyber security, xviii

Computer Emergency Response Team Coordination Center (CERT/CC), 1, 83, 118

computer espionage, 11n; scenario, 11–12n

Computer Misuse Act (1990), 7, 62, 63, 64n

computer-related crime, 19. *See also* cyber crime

computer-related forgery, fraud, 19

Computer Security Institute, 30

contact point (24/7), 4, 24, 131n

content-related crimes, 19–20

Convention of the Protection of Human Rights and Fundamental Freedoms, 94

Convention of the Protection of Individuals with Regard to Automatic Processing of Personal Data, 94

Convention on Human Rights (1950), 79

Convention on Human Rights and Biomedicine (1997), 80

Convention on Mutual Legal Assistance (1959), 17

cooperation, formal: and investigating cyber crime, 54; vs. informal, 48–49, 58–59

copyright, violations of, 19

Council of Europe, xviii, xx, 12n; Committee of Experts on Crime in Cyberspace, 91; draft convention by, 91–94; Committee on Crime Problems, 91; Convention No. 108, 88; Convention of the Protection of Human Rights and Fundamental Freedoms, 94; Convention of the Protection of Individuals

with Regard to Automatic Processing of Personal Data, 94; Convention on Mutual Legal Assistance of 1959, 17; Cybercrime Convention. *See* Cybercrime Convention; legal framework, 124–125; Recommendation of 1989, 18, 19
critical infrastructure protection, xix-xx
Croatia, 96
Cukoo's Egg, 11n
Curador, 7
cyber attack: definition, 10n; sophistication of, 100
cyber crime: active defense, 67; and business interests, 36, 38–39; and criminal law, 15, 16; definition of, 18, 88; evidence, 3, 91; extent of problem, 1–2; four categories of, 94; information on, 101, 104–105; information technology, 41–42; investigating, 35–36, 53–54; jursidiction, 33–35; and law enforcement, vx, 90; passive defense, 66–67; prevention of, 49–51, 52–55; problem assessment, 30–31; reporting of, 27–28, 32–33, 118–119; scenario, international, 69–70; serious offenses, 66; standard of proof, 62; surveys, 30; threat of, 31; tracking of, 2; transnational nature of, 90; types of, 40; vigilantism, 67–68; vs. espionage, warfare, 3–4; vulnerability to, 99, 101–103

Cybercrime Convention (CCC), xviii, xix, xxi, xxii, 5, 13, 15, 16, 34, 88; amendments to, 25; Articles of, 20–24; Chapter II, 20; CIA offenses, 19; content-related crimes, 19–20; copyright and related violations, 19; and First Amendment, 95–96; hate-speech protocol, 95–96; investigative measures, 24; and IT advancement, 25; jurisdiction provisions, 20; and mutual legal assistance, 18; parties to, 16; pending U.S. ratification of, 116; procedural law provisions, 20–22; purpose, 16–18; scope of, 18; substantive law provisions, 19–20
cyber crime model, 41–42
cyber espionage, 3
cyber forensics, 119
cyber incidents: reporting of, 118–119
cyber security, xv; agreements, 74–75; bilateral agreements, 2, 49, 52; bilateral cooperation, xx, xxi, 2, 5, 9, 43, 45–46; borderless nature of, 65, 112; CERTs, xviii; constraints on, xvii; cooperation, importance of, xii, xiii, xiv; definition of, 44; domestic cooperation, 44–45; domestic sovereignty, 120; formal agreements, 52; government's role in, 109–110, 112, 123; ideal cooperative arrangement, 69–73; ideal cooperative model, 75; industry

Information Society and Freedom, Security, and Justice program, xviii; "legal area," 87; personal data protection, 79–91, 81–87; Privacy Working Group, 92; treaty framework, 79
European Union Treaty, 82
European Working Party, 82
Explore, 10n
extradition, 22, 23, 46

FATF. *See* Financial Action Task Force
Federal Bureau of Investigation (FBI), 6, 7, 117; Computer Intrusion Squad, 30; Legal Attaches, 8
Financial Action Task Force (FATF), xix, 52
FIRST. *See* Forum of Incident Response and Security Teams
First Amendment: conflict with legal conventions, 95–96
Fluffi Bunni, 113
forensics center, 127–128
Forum of Incident Response and Security Teams (FIRST), 118, 130n
France, 85, 96
Freedom of Information Act, 117–118

gambling, 20
Germany, 9, 96; privacy right, 82
G-Force Pakistan, 113
Global Internet Liberty Campaign, 92
Goodman, Seymour E., xxii, 125
governance of Internet, xiii-xiv

government: role in cyber security, 109–110, 112, 123
"government time," 106
Gray, Raphael, 7
Greece, 82
Group of 8 (G-8), xviii, xx, 91; bilateral cooperation efforts, 5; law enforcement initiatives, 4–5; members, 12n; 24/7 network, 4, 24, 131n; security cooperation, xix; Subgroup on High-Tech Crime, 4, 5, 116, 131n

hacking, 113; examples, 6, 31, 63
Hamre, John, xxiii
hate speech, 95–96
hijacking, maritime, 34–35
Ho, Peter, 60
"honey pot," 108
Hong Kong, 125
human rights, 72–73
Hungary, 8, 84

ICAO. *See* International Civil Aviation Organization
ICC. *See* International Chamber of Commerce
ICRA. *See* Internet Content Rating Association
IDS. *See* intrusion detection systems
IETF. *See* Internet Engineering Task Force
ILOVEYOU virus, 7, 10n, 59
IMB. *See* International Maritime Bureau
informal cooperation: and investigating cyber crime, 54; vs. formal, 48–49

traffic data, 21
transnational governance, xxiii, 129; cyber security, 120; formal cooperation, 120–121; inter-agency coordination, 122–123; scope, 121

UNESCO, 92
United Kingdom, 7, 9, 117
United Nations, 121; Convention on the Suppression of Unlawful Acts against the Safety of Mari-time Navigation, 34, 35; Cov-enant on Civil and Polital Rights, 94
United States: interagency coordi-nation, 117–118; public-private coordination, 118–119; sover-eignty reservations to CCC, 68–69
University of California, Berkeley, 11n
U.S. Department of Defense, 118, 126–127; Computer Forensics Laboratory, 119; intrusions into, 11n
U.S. Department of Energy, 118
U.S. Department of Justice, 91, 117; Computer Crime and Intellectual Property Security, 115–116
U.S. Department of State, 2, 116
USA Patriot Act (2001), 59

Vatik, Michael, xxi
Venice Declaration, 85
Vienna Convention on the Law of Treaties, 18

vigilantism, 67–68
viruses. *See also* hacking: resulting damage of, 1

Wank Worm, 130n
watchdog groups, 27, 28
WIPO. *See* World Intellectual Property Organization
wiretapping, 92, 93
Worcester, Massachusetts, 113
Working Party, 88
World Conference Data Protec-tion of 2001, 85
World Intellectual Property Orga-nization (WIPO), 19
worms, 31, 130n

xenophobic material, 20

Yahoo!, 6, 31, 96
Young Intelligence Hackers Against Terrorism (YIHAT), 113

Zubeck, Katherine, xxiii

ABOUT THE AUTHORS

Prakash Ambegaonkar is president of the Bridging Nations Foundation and a senior associate at the Center for Strategic and International Studies (CSIS) in Washington, D.C.

Seymour E. Goodman is professor of international affairs at the Sam Nunn School of International Affairs, as well as professor of computing in the College of Computing, at Georgia Institute of Technology in Atlanta.

John J. Hamre is president and CEO of the Center for Strategic and International Studies (CSIS). He is a former U.S. deputy secretary of defense.

Henrik Kaspersen is the director of the Computer-Law Institute at Vrije Universiteit in Amsterdam, The Netherlands. From 1997 to 2001, he chaired the committee that negotiated and drafted the Council of Europe Cybercrime Convention.

Gordon N. Lederman is an associate in the National Security Law and Policy Practice Group at Arnold & Porter in Washington, D.C.

James A. Lewis is director of the Technology and Public Policy Program at the Center for Strategic and International Studies (CSIS) in Washington, D.C.

Charles Lim Aeng Cheng is principal senior state counsel of the Law Reform and Revision Division of the Attorney-General's Chambers in Singapore.

Robert S. Litt is a partner at Arnold & Porter in Washington, D.C. He was formerly with the U.S. Department of Justice.

Nobuo Miwa is the executive director of LAC Co. Ltd., and the head of the LAC Security Laboratory in Tokyo.

Pottengal Mukundan is director of Commercial Crime Services at the International Chamber of Commerce in London.

Stefano Rodotà is president of the Italian Data Protection Authority in Rome.

Michael Vatis was the director of the Institute for Security Technology Studies at Dartmouth College in Hanover, N.H., at the time of this writing. He is also a lawyer with Fried, Frank, Harris, Shriver & Jacobson.

Katherine Crotty Zuback is with the Department of Defense and was a visiting fellow at CSIS at the time of this writing.